MAKING SHOTS

Tee to Green

GAME IMPROVEMENT LIBRARY™

CREDITS

MAKING SHOTS
TEE TO GREEN

Tom Carpenter
Director of Book Development

Julie Cisler, Gina Germ
Book Design & Production

Michele Teigen
Senior Book Development Coordinator

Steve Hosid
Instruction Editor/Photographer

Steve Ellis
Editor

Ward Clayton   **Leo McCullagh**
Bob Combs   **Mike Mueller**
PGA TOUR

Special thanks to the following golf course for allowing us to shoot on location:
The Country Club DC Ranch: Scottsdale, Arizona

Acknowledgements
"To the members of the PGA TOUR Partners Club I meet at tournaments around the country: Your questions, comments and support help create articles and books that truly reflect the needs of our outstanding membership."

—*Steve Hosid*

8 7 6 5 4 3 2 1 / 09 08 07 06 05 04 03 02
ISBN 1-58159-174-8
PGA TOUR Partners Club
12301 Whitewater Drive
Minnetonka, Minnesota 55343

ABOUT THE AUTHOR/ PHOTOGRAPHER

Steve Hosid is instruction editor, contributing writer and photographer for *PGA TOUR Partners* magazine and the Club's Game Improvement Library. He is co-author of *The Complete Idiot's Guide to Healthy Stretching* (with Chris Verna), and *Golf for Everybody* (with Brad Brewer, former director of The Arnold Palmer Golf Academies), and has collaborated on books with LPGA star Michelle McGann and tennis player MaliVai Washington.

Steve is a graduate of the University of Southern California. He and his wife, Jill, live with two non-golfing Borzoi Wolfhounds on the 13th hole at Arnold Palmer's Bay Hill Club & Lodge in Orlando, Florida.

PGA TOUR Partners Club President Tom Lehman (standing) with Steve Hosid.

CONTENTS

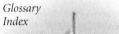

INTRODUCTION

This is the book every golfer wants to have for working on their own game. With the subject matter arranged in alphabetical order, like an encyclopedia, you can turn to the exact page to find the information for a particular phase of your game or technique. If you only want backswing help, for example, you'll find it in the B-section. It's like having Tom Lehman and Martin Hall ready and waiting to help with just the information you seek, whenever you need them.

For each subject we've included shotmaking checklists to quickly help you zone in on the important aspects of the shot: a positive way to program your mind for success. This is personal instruction, just as if Tom invited you inside the ropes for a *one-on-one* session. You get into the mind of a PGA TOUR professional, learning how he approaches that phase of the game and implements his keys for success.

Our Partners Club Game Improvement Library™ books are written in a conversational style, featuring loads of photos, to give you the feeling of being out on the course for *hands-on* instruction. We don't waste pages writing about the theory of the golf swing because that wastes your time. You want to improve as quickly as possible.

I first met Tom Lehman after he won the 1996 British Open and became President of the PGA TOUR Partners Club. Over the years we worked together on instruction articles for the magazine, as well as some books, and became good friends. He thinks like all of us *amateur golfers*, as you'll discover in the pages that follow. Tom is not overly technical. Instead he talks in terms that you'll find easy to relate to.

Tom Lehman

I was a 1-handicap golfer during my college days at USC but have slipped to an 8. The information I learned from Tom and Martin has me back on track again. Just one example is how simply Tom works the ball. By pre-setting his grip either more left or right, and opening or closing his stance, he flawlessly controls each shot's shape. I won't even go into the complicated way I was originally taught, but trying it Tom's way lets me consistently control every shot shape from tee to green. I know you will improve too!

Most of this book was shot on location in Scottsdale, Arizona, at the Country Club at DC Ranch. It's Tom's home course.

I've written many books, but working with Tom Lehman on this one makes it very special. Enjoy what he has to say, and put it to good use out on the golf course.

Martin Hall has long been considered one of golf's top instructors. You've seen him on the Golf Channel and in all the Partners Club videos. Martin is an integral part of our Game Improvement books.

Once I attended a teaching symposium for club pros featuring Martin and some other recognizable names in golf instruction. The aim was to help the club instructors learn how to best teach their members.

One group was out on the practice range and the faculty demonstrated how they would help a student powerfully follow through impact correctly. Each instructor, except Martin, talked about the theory of what the student should do. When it was Martin's turn he put a ball on an old shaft ahead, slightly behind the golfer, and said, "Swing through impact and hit this ball off the shaft too!" It was so simple and effective. But best of all it was teaching *feeling* and not theory. Martin uses the same approach in this book. If improvement is your goal, get ready for lower scores!

Martin Hall

TOM'S 20 QUICK TIPS
A MAKING SHOTS SAMPLER

Here is a selection of key tips that you will find in this comprehensive shotmaking encyclopedia. For the first time, vital parts of the game are presented in alphabetical order, offering just the immediate information you need as a quick fix reference or for a leisurely read.

PLAY TO YOUR STRENGTHS

"Always play to your strengths! When I'm playing, my strategy centers around what I can do best, not what someone else can do."

"I'm a firm believer that high handicappers should take the long irons out of their bags and put in woods."

SUBSTITUTE CLUBS

"There are always ways to improve. The key is knowing what you are capable of and how you can improve upon that. Tom Lehman plays golf like Tom Lehman. Playing golf like Davis Love or Mike Reid is not going to work for me."

BE YOURSELF

WHEN OFFSET CAN HELP

"A little offset, which helps get your irons into the air, also tends to hook the ball. If your ball flight is normally a draw, then these clubs are not for you. But if your shots consistently bend to the right, offset can help the ball go a little straighter and even draw somewhat."

TOM'S COMPRESSION CHOICE

"Do you need to play a 100-compression ball? I don't use one! I play a 90."

"I feel my grip is balanced, although it's not a classically perfect grip by any means. The key is it works for me."

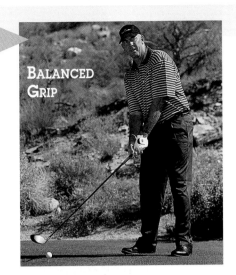

BALANCED GRIP

"Very important! There is no getting around the fact that, both physically and anatomically, you are not able to turn around a spine that is curved compared to a spine that is straight. Good posture allows you to consistently make a good turn around your spine."

GOOD POSTURE

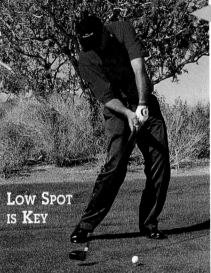
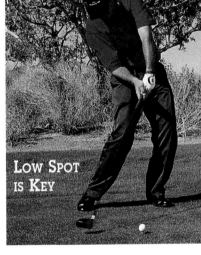

LOW SPOT IS KEY

"Placing the ball in the low spot of your swing **every time** helps you hit a solid shot **every time**."

"I play with a long thumb grip, but I used to play the short thumb when I was in high school and college. The longer thumb allows a longer swing with a little more wrist cock at the top of my backswing."

LONG THUMB GRIP

"If I feel uncomfortable at address, I'll back off the ball and try to be a little more specific with what I'm trying to do."

STAY IN CONTROL

PREPARE FOR SUCCESS

"There is nothing that replaces being properly prepared in your mind for hitting a quality golf shot."

LEAD YOUR MOVEMENT

"A good golfer's downswing begins like the delivery of a baseball pitcher. They lead their movement toward the plate with the left leg, and so do we."

"If I were to start teaching a beginner, the thing I would work on the hardest would be to get them into the right position at the top of the backswing. Once there, it's just a reaction to hit the ball."

TOP OF BACKSWING IS KEY

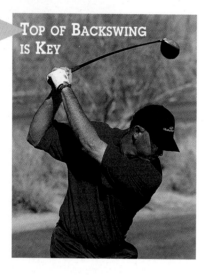

SMOOTH SWINGS

"Good players' swings look so smooth and effortless because their weight goes back and allows them to move the club a long way very easily."

THE BEST MISTAKE

"The best mistake you can make on the downswing is letting your weight go too far left."

WEDGES FOR ACCURACY

"Wedges and short irons are for accuracy, not distance."

"The best chippers have really good control over the trajectory."

CONTROL CHIPPING TRAJECTORY

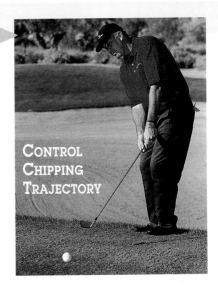

CHIPPING SAVES STROKES

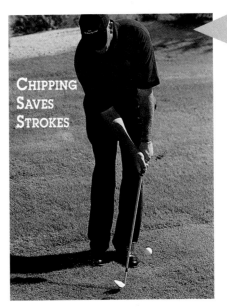

"Chipping is the easiest way for the average golfer to shave strokes from their scores."

"The weaker your grip when playing a wedge, the less hand action will be involved with the shot. The stronger your grip, the more your hands work through impact. The ball will curve more but your accuracy will be less consistent."

WEAK WEDGE GRIP

"As you putt, the butt of the club should be pointing toward your sternum on the backstroke and through-stroke."

CLUB BUTT TOWARD STERNUM

A COURTYARD CONVERSATION

After finishing their work on *Making Shots—Tee to Green*, Tom Lehman and his friend and author, Steve Hosid, spent some time in the DC Ranch Golf Club's hacienda courtyard. In the shadow of Pinnacle Peak and overlooking Phoenix's Valley of the Sun, they discussed golf's impact on Tom's life, his views on helping golfers of all levels improve, and his future as a golf-course architect.

Steve Hosid: Tom, I once asked Arnold Palmer what golf meant to his life, and his answer was that golf has allowed him to meet people he would have never met, created business opportunities and gave him the ability to help others. How would you answer that question?

Tom Lehman: It has meant so many different things, but foremost golf has always been fun for me. It's one of the greatest ways to spend time with your friends or your family doing something that is really enjoyable.

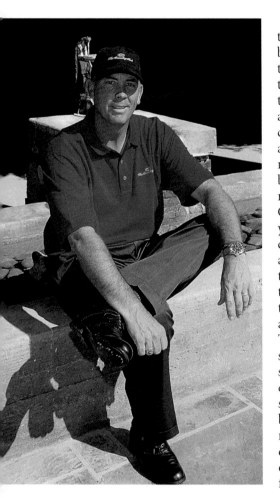

Beyond that, golf has been a great tool, teaching me to work hard and be committed, and, as a result, become self-motivated. Golf teaches you how to deal with adversity and triumph—the good times as well as the bad. This may sound strange, but dealing with success may be even more difficult than dealing with failure.

I'm a more complete person because golf has provided me an opportunity to grow as a person.

Steve: Given the choice, I'm sure you prefer having to deal with the success, but what if all of this hadn't worked out for you? Let's say that you never developed the talent or interest to play on the PGA TOUR. What other career options would you have explored?

Tom: Being the head basketball coach at a major university would have been a very fulfilling way to live my life. I would have chosen to work my way into a situation where I could ultimately be involved with a quality, high-level program focused on reaching the NCAA's Final Four and, ultimately, winning the national championship.

Steve: You did win a national championship—the 1996 British Open at Royal Lytham and St. Anne's. What is there about winning a major that seems to validate a professional golfer's career, even if they have been successful on TOUR?

Tom: Winning a major definitely puts you into a different category, or at least others see you as being in a different category. Over the years, there have been many great players who never won majors. In fact, they may have even been better players than those who have won them. But the result is that your career as a golfer is enhanced and you find yourself put on a pedestal where otherwise you wouldn't be.

Winning a major is one thing, but it's also important to do other things along the way so that it won't be regarded as a fluke. Winning several other tournaments and playing on Ryder Cup and President Cup teams are what elevates you in the perception of the golfing public.

Steve: Winning a major opens a lot of other opportunities for you, but it also increases the demands on your time. Overall, is that good or bad?

Tom: Not all of what comes from winning a major can be classified as good. What it does provide is a lot more opportunities to say yes or no.

Steve: Throughout your career, you have hit many memorable shots. Is there one that stands out?

Tom: During the 1995 Ryder Cup, Corey Pavin and I were playing an alternate-shot match against Nick Faldo and Colin Montgomerie. We were tied going to the 18th hole. In a driving rainstorm, I hit a 5-iron 205 yards on the green. It was cold and miserable, but that shot helped us win the match.

Steve: Tom, if you were granted one mulligan, my guess is the shot you would cash it in for would be the shot you hit into the water late in the final round of the 1997 U.S. Open at Congressional Country Club.

Tom: You've got that right. I would definitely like to have the mulligan and use it back on the 17th fairway of the U.S. Open at Congressional. (Author's note: Tom had joined Bobby Jones as the only players to have led the U.S. Open after three rounds three straight years. But on Sunday, hitting into the water on the 71st hole eliminated Tom's chance of winning. He finished third, two strokes behind Ernie Els.)

Steve: Knowing that golf-course architecture is one of your passions, do you feel being a world-class player helps or hinders becoming a world-class designer?

Tom: History's great golf course designers—Donald Ross *(Pinehurst #2)*, Harry Colt *(Pine Valley)* and Alister Mackenzie *(Augusta National)*—shared one very important element: they understood both sides of the coin. They understood the engineering side and were also good players.

Conversely, you may be a good player but unless you understand the engineering aspects, all your golfing talent won't do you any good. We have many excellent course designers today. But I feel there are still opportunities for someone to step in and become a current-day Mackenzie or Ross, combining great strategic aspects with the esthetics and design of truly great courses. That's my goal as I continue to develop as a designer.

Steve: I'm giving you what could be the most perfect piece of land. It has virtually everything a designer would want— mountains and desert, forests, oceanfront and lakes. How would you envision taking advantage of all of these elements and carving out a truly great golf course?

Tom: Great courses have a certain aura about them, a certain ambiance. When you step out on the ground, you know and feel you are someplace special. Maybe it's the ocean. Maybe it's just the beautiful setting with trees or mountains or rivers.

For instance, when you go to Winged Foot or Shinnecock Hills you know you are someplace special. My friend Lyle Anderson, who owns Desert Highland and Desert Mountain, and Loch Lomand in Scotland, told me when I first started designing golf courses, "If you want to be known as a great designer then do projects that start with great pieces of land."

That's great advice because Mackenzie didn't build any great courses in the middle of the Bonneville Salt Flats. He went to the coast and built them on the ocean or in the middle of redwood forests. You are a step ahead of the game if you start with great land like that.

Steve: There has been tremendous development of outstanding equipment in recent years. But are the amateurs you play with in pro-ams benefiting from it?

Tom: Lasting improvement in your game can only come from one way—hard work. If you are trying to buy a game, you can buy maybe a few more yards or a little less slice or hook. But you will not develop into a good player unless you work at it.

Steve: But what can the average golfer do who can't devote the hours to work on their games?

Tom: Let me clarify that a little to give some suggestions. The one thing you should try to avoid is limiting a practice session to only once a week.

Golf relies on muscle memory, and spending even a little time every day having a club in your hands goes a long way to developing a consistent game. Even if you can't get to the course, you can work on some things in your yard or even hold a club working on your grip while watching television. That mirror in the hallway is a great aid to check your positions and posture.

My ideal suggestion is to try to carve out a half hour a day during your lunchtime to putt or chip or hit a few balls. The results will prove you'll be better off doing that than doing one big session once a week.

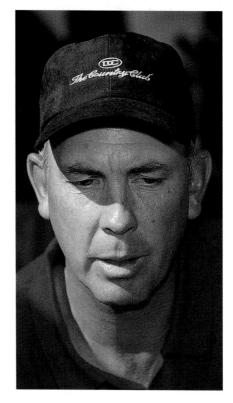

TOOLS OF THE GAME

The Rules of Golf allow a maximum of 14 clubs in your bag. These are your tools! They are going to help you shoot lower scores, so they better perform. You need only those clubs in your golf bag that can do the job for you. Choose them wisely, based on your ability and for the type of course you will be playing.

Tom's Club Choices

1 Driver

- **7 degrees of loft, 110-gram graphite shaft**

My shaft is heavy for graphite. In fact, it's almost as heavy as a steel shaft. I prefer a shaft that is very stiff in the handle with a weaker tip down by the hosel. This provides a little more "kick" when the clubhead comes into the ball, which I've always liked.

The kick gets the drive spinning more. That's ideal for me because I launch the ball a little low, but it's ill suited for a golfer who naturally launches the ball higher. Remember, choose clubs that will enhance *your* game, not because someone else is using them.

2 Fairway Woods

- **3-wood—17 degrees**

- **4-wood**

While some professionals prefer to carry three wedges, I usually prefer to carry three fairway woods. The clubs are carefully selected for each round during a tournament based on the course and weather conditions.

A 5-wood and a 1-iron are clubs I consider to be on the "bubble" and can be exchanged for other clubs depending on my specific needs. For example, a 60-degree wedge goes in the bag when I'm playing a course like Muirfield Village, with its steep banks and bunkers, which requires getting the ball up quicker.

8 Irons

- **2, 3, 4, 5, 6, 7, 8, 9**

2 Wedges

- **Pitching wedge**

- **56-degree sand wedge**

1 Putter

This choice is entirely up to you. One trip to the golf specialty store or your local course pro shop reveals just how many styling options are available. The key is to test several of them. If one feels right, helps you line up properly, feels good during your swing and gives you the confidence needed to sink more putts then go with it.

HIGH HANDICAPPERS: PUT IN MORE WOODS

I talked my dad into taking two of his irons (2- and 3-iron) out of his bag and substituting a 7-wood and 9-wood. Long irons are far more difficult to play, and your 2-iron is going to get you in trouble.

Fairway woods make it easier to launch a ball in the air because of their mass compared to a long iron. Just make your normal swing, even from a bad lie.

Clubs can enhance your game by compensating for some swing flaws. Depending on your specific needs, several choices are available ranging from cast, forged, perimeter weighted and offset. Golf specialty stores or your local pro will let you test variations of all of these. Never buy clubs without first evaluating them for your own needs.

MIDDLE HANDICAPPERS: CLUBHEAD SPEED IS THE KEY

Your club selection depends on the amount of clubhead speed your swing is capable of delivering. Compare the distance and accuracy of your long irons to those of the fairway woods. Only the champions should make it into your bag.

At this level, you will also benefit from perimeter weighting, which places more weight toward the bottom of the clubhead. A little offset can also help, if you tend to slice.

ACCURACY CONTROL

    Golf is a target sport. Watch your scores improve as you increase the percentage of balls that land on your targets. Everyone can get lucky occasionally, but consistently identifying and then reaching targets is the true measure of improvement.

    Accuracy requires both mental and physical preparation. While target alignment plays a huge role, shots from the various elements of the game—long, scoring zone and putting—have their own special accuracy requirements. The checklists for each category will help keep or get you back on target. You'll also find more in-depth information under the alphabetical listing for each element.

ACCURACY: LONG GAME

✔CHECKLIST
LONG GAME ACCURACY
✔ Specific targets.
✔ Posture.
✔ Ball position.
✔ Tempo.
✔ Balance.

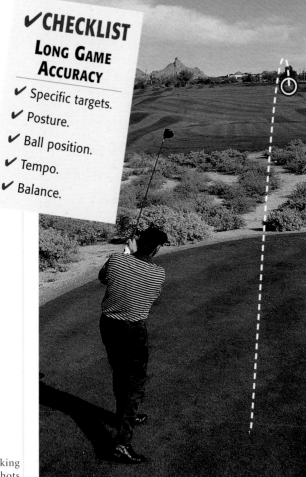

SPECIFIC TARGETS

    If you are thrilled with just hitting the fairway, the first course of action is selecting and visualizing smaller, more defined targets. Better golfers limit the size of their targets to avoid trouble or achieve the best line to the hole.

    Time for a confession and then a tip. I've never been good at picking out just a spot on the ground to hit to. Another solution had to be found. In my case, focusing on a spot a long way out and on the same target line works best. I look for trees, a water tower, a building or a hill to help pick out the perfect line. Then I visualize the ball flying along that line.

Here, Tom selects the tree as a target. His accuracy improves when his targets are farther away as opposed to a spot on the ground.

POSTURE

Accuracy comes from being able to set and then maintain consistent posture angles throughout the golf swing. Standing straight and then bending from the waist allows you to swing around a consistent body axis.

A common mistake is bending over too far and curving your spine. You have to make swing compensations to get back to the ball, and that's a poison pill for accuracy.

Posture must be on your checklist as something to think about while setting up for a shot. Visualize a line extending down from your shoulders through your knees and into the top of your feet. This helps you verify you are **standing up** to the ball correctly. Additional posture help can be found on pages 114-115.

BALL POSITION

For accuracy, the ball must be positioned at the bottom of your swing arc.

For this accuracy checklist, think of your swing as a circle that has both a high and low point. Your ball must be positioned at the low point—or bottom—of the swing arc for the clubhead to be square to the target line at impact. The key to accuracy is positioning the ball at this low point of the swing for each shot you hit, not just getting lucky and finding it every now and then.

For the longest club in my bag—the driver—that low point is opposite my left heel. Consistent accuracy demands placing it there every time I address the ball. Vary the position either slightly forward or back and the clubface arrives at the ball either open to the target line or closed.

Stand up tall and bend from the waist. You should be able to draw an imaginary line from your shoulders down through your knees into the top of your feet.

In either case, the ball will start away from the target line. I'll demonstrate exact ball positions (*see Ball Position*) on page 33.

A

TEMPO

Think of your swing's tempo as its electrical transformer for accuracy. The only time maximum current or energy should be applied is through the impact zone. Any jerky power surge at the wrong time and accuracy is fried; some part of your body will move out of position.

We'll deal more with timing and tempo later *(see the Timing and Tempo listing)*. But for accuracy checklist purposes use the three pendulum photos below for positive visualization. Can you think of anything with more consistent tempo than a pendulum?

To instill tempo in your swing, try this drill before teeing off or starting a session on the practice range. Grip the club naturally and then place its butt against your sternum.

Holding the club tightly against your sternum, rotate into the backswing position until your back faces the target. Say "one" as you make this smooth motion.

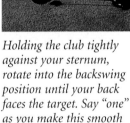

Continue holding the club against the sternum and rotate smoothly down and through until your chest faces the target as you say "two." Now repeat this motion back and forth as you count rhythmically.

BALANCE

Last on the long game accuracy checklist is balance. Think in these terms: A swing made while you are properly balanced will follow a natural path without compensations, but a swing made out of balance is subject to how you try to recover. Balance truly is a key to accuracy.

Proper weight transfer during your swing encourages good balance (see *Weight Shift* too). Problems arise when your weight goes to the wrong side at the wrong time. Try the drill at right before teeing off or hitting a long club. The motion will instill proper balance in your swing.

On the backswing, transfer your weight over to the side away from the target, storing up energy. As a result, right-handed golfers should be able to balance on their right leg and left-handed golfers on their left. Lifting the opposite leg verifies correct weight transfer. If you can't lift it, the weight transfer has not occurred.

On the downswing, transfer your weight from the side away from the target to the side closest to the target. As a result, right-handed golfers should be able to balance on their left leg and left-handers on their right. Try lifting the opposite leg to check your balance.

ACCURACY: SCORING ZONE

Once you're within range of reaching the green, accuracy should be your number-one goal. Off-line shots result in needless extra strokes to scramble back into position on the green.

For accuracy, your clubface must be square to the target line (90 degrees) when the face meets the ball. Even a small deviation will send the ball considerably off target.

Square

Closed

Open

When a clubface impacts the ball only a fraction open or closed, the ball travels considerably more off line than you might think. The farther the ball travels from the impact point, the wider the target deviation angle gets.

✔**CHECKLIST**
SCORING ZONE ACCURACY

Using this list, along with Martin Hall's helpful tips and drills, will focus you on the most important factors for developing accuracy in the scoring zone.

✔ Neutral grip.

✔ Clubface position hip high.

✔ Clubhead position—top of backswing.

✔ Swing path for hips and shoulders.

NEUTRAL GRIP

The simple act of gripping a club plays a vital role in the position of your clubface at impact. Use the self-diagnosis chart below to help identify grip problems that may be destroying your chance for accuracy before you even swing the club. The V's of both hands formed by the thumb and index finger are the determining factor.

GRIP SELF-DIAGNOSIS

WEAK GRIP

V's point toward the left side of the body for right-handed players and the right side of the body for left-handed players.

Ball Flight Direction

Usually to the right because the clubface is open at impact.

Distance Control

Weak shot that will not have enough velocity to reach the target.

Compensation

Swinging across the ball, trying to steer it more to the left. This makes the situation grimmer as the open clubface slices across the ball at impact from outside the target line.

STRONG GRIP

V's point toward, or even outside, the right shoulder for a right-handed player. Left-handed players will find the V's pointed to their left shoulder.

Ball Flight Direction

Usually sharply to the left as a result of a closed clubface at impact.

Distance Control

Shot will be lower and hotter, making distance control difficult.

Compensation

Swinging in-to-out in a vain attempt to steer the ball toward the left.

DRILL

CLAP HANDS DRILL

A proven method for improving the basics of your game is to rely on familiar movements for developing both mental and muscle memory. Simply clapping your hands develops the feeling of a neutral grip, with the left hand on one side of the club and the right hand on the other.

Rest the club against the center of your body and position the palms of your hands so they face each other as you spread them apart. Clap your hands together and then take your grip, creating the same feeling of the palms facing each other.

A

CLUBFACE POSITION HIP HIGH

Martin Hall suggests using a yardstick's flat side to practice attaining the correct hip-high positions.

An outstanding method for developing correct hip-high clubhead positions for both the backswing and past impact utilizes a simple yardstick. I put a bit of black tape on it for emphasis here, but under that added "glitz" it is just a basic yardstick with two flat wide-side edges.

Two important points to remember for consistently positioning the club correctly are shown and explained in the photos below.

On the backswing and past impact, the club must reach two critical hip-high points correctly. Any other position means the swing deviated from an accuracy-producing swing plane.

INCORRECT CLUB POSITIONING

Remember that when a club is parallel to the ground at hip height it should also be parallel to the target line. But in these two photos showing common mistakes, it's not. In both cases, the yardstick shows the correct position.

Clubhead inside the line. *A faulty take-away brought the clubhead back too abruptly along an inside swing path.*

Clubhead outside the line. *A hands and arms only take-away is the culprit in this too-steep swing plane.*

HIP-HIGH BACKSWING POSITION   HIP-HIGH PAST IMPACT POSITION

Any time the shaft reaches a parallel-to-the-ground position, it must also be parallel to the target line. After gripping the yardstick with your palms on the wide flat sides, those sides should be pointing straight up and down at both hip-high positions.

CLUBHEAD POSITION—TOP OF BACKSWING

Training aids don't have to be expensive to achieve the desired results. I'm using a badminton racket to illustrate the correct accuracy-producing clubhead position at the top of your short game backswing.

CORRECT POSITIONS

Notice that the racket and the clubface are both set up 90 degrees to the target line at address. To return to this square position at impact, good golfers achieve the correct position at the top of their backswing.

As the clubhead reaches the hip-high position, the racket and clubfaces are vertical to the ground.

HOOKING POSITION

This is the incorrect position that contributes to hooking. Instead of just the edges pointing down the target line, the racket and clubface are shut and facing the camera. The clubface will close down on the ball at impact, causing a hook.

SLICING POSITION

Hardly any of the racket's face is visible at the top of the backswing. Both the racket and clubface are correctly positioned, and only the edges are pointed down the target line. Compare these photos with the incorrect photos at right to become familiar with correct clubhead position at the top of your backswing.

This incorrect position causes slicing. The racket and clubface are open and laid back to the target line at the backswing's top. When the clubface points to the golfer, as in this example, it will slice across the ball at impact.

A

SWING PATH FOR HIPS AND SHOULDERS

Assuming you hit the ball consistently in the center of the clubface, accuracy then depends on where the face is at impact. This is where shoulders and hips enter the picture: They control the swing path, which controls the face position.

Try the next two drills to work on consistently swinging along the same correct path. Accuracy is not derived from improvisation as you try recovering from improper positions. It develops from continually repeating correct techniques.

DRILL

SWING PATH: CLUB ON SHOULDERS DRILL

Use a long shaft. But you can use a broomstick or spare shaft held to your chest by a bungee cord wrapped around the shaft and your back. This shaft is your shoulder position indicator.

Using a target line on the ground, address the ball and make a complete backswing. Notice that shoulder rotation brought the shaft to a 90-degree angle to the target line. Make sure your hip-high and top-of-backswing positions are correct.

The key to this drill is timing the downswing so your shoulders and the shaft will be parallel to the target line when you hit the ball. Your hips will be slightly open to the line, allowing room for your arms to swing through.

INCORRECT SHOULDER POSITIONS

PUSHED SHOTS

If your shoulder position looks like this at impact—with the target side of the shaft pointing to the right—you probably push your shots to the right. Use this drill:

• Swing slowly.

• Check your backswing positions.

• Time the downswing so the shoulders are parallel to the target line at impact.

PULLED SHOTS

If your shoulders and the target side of the shaft point to the left at impact, you most likely pull your shots to the left. The cure for both pulled and pushed shots is the same: parallel shoulders at impact. To correct the problem, use the same steps as shown at left.

SWING PATH: FOUR-STEP DRILL

Straight, accurate shots will be your reward once you use this drill to train your muscles and mind to reach the correct position at the top of every backswing.

STEP 1

Lift the club and lay it on your right shoulder. Left-handers lay it on your left shoulder.

STEP 2

With the club on your shoulder, turn your body to the right (left-handers turn to the left).

STEP 3

Stretch your hands and club out and away from your body. You are now in the correct position at the top of your scoring zone backswing.

STEP 4

Swing down and through the ball.

A

ACCURACY: PUTTING

Becoming an accurate putter requires a checklist of its own. While they are listed here, more detailed information can be found in the section on putting (page 117). An accuracy tip used by SENIOR PGA TOUR player Dave Stockton since he was a young boy is shown here.

(page 117)

✔ CHECKLIST

PUTTING ACCURACY

✔ Correct line to the hole.

✔ Alignment should be to the direction the ball starts out.

✔ Eyes should be over or slightly inside the ball.

✔ Putting style is optional, however the blade should always contact the ball at a 90-degree angle to the target line to start the ball on the correct target line.

✔ Back of left hand goes toward the target through contact.

DRILL

DAVE STOCKTON: LEFT HAND TO THE TARGET

Dave Stockton considers his left hand to be his direction hand and wants it to lead the way through his putting stroke. Try this drill his father taught him, to improve your putting accuracy.

Have a friend hold up a club so that it touches the emblem on the back of your glove. Then the club should be backed up on the same line about three inches.

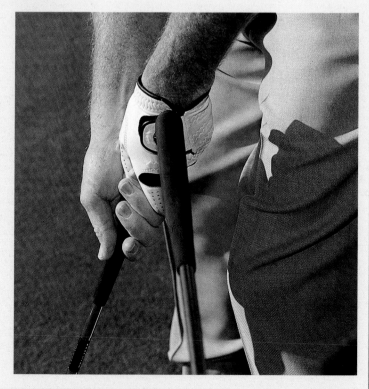

Stroke the ball so that the emblem again comes into contact with the club. Ideally, you want to go lower with the wrist as Dave has. This drill trains your muscle memory to have the back of the left hand go toward your target past impact, ensuring that the clubface will be square.

ADDRESS

If someone told you that to become a good golfer you need to excel in geometry, chances are your clubs would never see the light of day. Geometry is probably the last subject you think about when heading out to the course.

Don't worry. We won't bog you down with memorizing the Pythagorean Theorem and its applications. Just be aware that golf is a geometric sport with angles and arcs. But becoming a good golfer does require understanding one specific geometric application: the 90-degree angle.

This 90-degree angle, formed by the lines representing the target line and clubface, must be created at setup and replicated at impact if you want to improve your game.

SETTING THE GAP

Drawing a line from the ball toward the target is easy, but golfers play from the side and this is where the 90-degree angle comes in. It's the angle your clubface and the target line must form at address and impact.

Always check your GAP.

Remember. The ball starts in the direction the clubface is moving, so you want the clubface moving down the target line through impact. Change that angle and the ball goes off line.

✔ CHECKLIST
GAP ADDRESS

✔ Grip.

✔ Alignment.

✔ Posture.

Use this checklist to help set up properly every time. Think of it as setting the GAP to program your mind as you set up to the ball. More information about all three can be found in their own alphabetical sections.

GRIP

The first thing good instructors will do is watch how you grip the club. Even before you make the swing, they will already know a great deal about the quality of your game. Nothing destroys your potential to improve more than an incorrect grip.

Don't just take your grip for granted; be sure to monitor it as you address the ball. The key is the direction the V's, formed by your thumb and forefinger of each hand, are pointing.

A good grip is the first step to a good address.

Look over Tom's shoulder. Notice that the tees placed in the V's of both his hands are pointing to the right/center portion of his body. You can change a ball's path by strengthening the grip so the V's point more to the right, or weakening it so the V's point more to the left.

- *V's pointing to the right side indicate a strong grip and a tendency to draw the ball (right-to-left).*

- *V's pointing to the left side indicate a weak grip and a tendency to fade the ball (left-to-right).*

A

ALIGNMENT

The 90-degree angle comes into play here. As the photo shows, Tom has aligned his body so that the clubface forms a 90-degree angle with the target line. When good players begin to have a problem, it can often be traced to an alignment issue.

Good players are consistent because they take the time to align their bodies properly to the target. Put your feet on a line parallel to the target line, unless you are planning to bend the ball flight in either direction.

As a result, you will often see PGA TOUR professionals practice on the range with a club that is parallel to the target line placed by their feet.

Under Alignment, you will find additional help and information on how to properly align your shoulders, hips and knees to the target line.

TOM'S SHOTMAKING TIPS

Uncomfortable at Address

Do you occasionally feel so uncomfortable at address that you fidget around trying to adjust things? Maybe the grip or something else feels wrong. That happens to me, too, and the usual reason is that something in my vision is causing me to feel that the shot's angle is off.

When I'm uncomfortable at address, I'll back off the ball and try to be a little more specific about what I'm trying to do. If I still feel uncomfortable, then I simplify things by concentrating on setting up 90 degrees to the target line.

1 Line the club up to the target.

2 Set your feet parallel to where the ball and club are being aimed.

3 The confidence of knowing you're square to the target eliminates discomfort.

POSTURE

Good posture at address allows Tom to rotate around a straight spine angle as he swings the club back. When you can maintain good posture throughout the swing, you don't have to make compensations just to get back to the ball.

Earlier we placed posture on the accuracy checklist, and we repeated it for this address checklist. I can't put enough emphasis on how important posture is to a repeatable golf swing. If you can set the proper spine angle, you can maintain it throughout the swing.

Many people make the mistake of bending over too much, believing that this puts them in a good athletic position at address when in fact it has doomed their swing. Result: They will bob up and down during the swing.

Remember to stand tall, as I am above, with a little flex in your knees. The bending occurs at the waist. That's the reason I maintain my posture, as you can see in the accompanying action photo.

ALIGNMENT

When you work on your target alignment, make sure your body is parallel to your target line as well as your feet. All too often a slice is caused by an outside-to-in swing as a result of shoulders that are inadvertently set up pointing to the left when the rest of the body is aligned properly.

Improper alignment is the first thing I look for when my game gets off a little. Sometimes I like to practice with a club placed on the ground and parallel to the target line. This provides a good reference point to make sure your shoulders, hips and knees are also aligned properly.

CHECK YOUR ALIGNMENT

1 Tom lays a club on the ground parallel to the target line, then begins setting up by aligning his feet. Next, he takes another club and holds it on the front of his shoulders. Notice this club is parallel to the club on the ground.

2 Tom places the club on the front of his hips, checking to make sure they are also parallel to the club on the ground.

3 With the club placed on the front of his knees, Tom is verifying they are also parallel to the target line.

TOM SOLVES THE MYSTERY

Do you sometimes say, "I hit it great on the range but when I get to the course something happens"?

On the practice range, it's easy to align yourself properly and hit ball after ball accurately because everything is set up on a 90-degree grid. But once you are out on the course alignment can suffer because of subconscious things you do to compensate for angles your brain detects.

For example, a tee box is rectangular in shape, but say that on a specific hole the markers line up directly toward a fairway bunker. This may cause you to aim slightly left to get the ball on the fairway. With those lines off the tee aiming you toward the bunker, it's difficult to mentally block them out, and subconsciously you make slight alignment adjustments that negatively affect your swing. In cases like this, I find I have to aim way left or right to compensate.

A

BACKSWING

Visualizing just five tips can develop a good backswing. Positively programming your brain with the right thoughts and images pays huge dividends, eliminating all the negative pictures that produce unsatisfactory results.

On the practice range, sweep out the old swing thoughts clogging up your mind. Try visualizing a large sweeping arc, and program your mind and muscles for a good, wide swing plane. Out on the course, think about these five tips during your pre-shot routine, and trace the wide swing arc with your clubhead during your practice swings.

✔ CHECKLIST
BACKSWING

✔ Think about swinging the clubhead.

✔ Think about the swing arc the clubhead must follow.

✔ Try to create that arc with your clubhead.

✔ Keep your head and spine centered.

✔ Try to make as big an arc on the backswing as you possibly can.

WIDE SWING ARC

Tom's one-piece take-away creates a wide swing arc that produces consistent accuracy and power.

I start my swing—after a slight forward press to initiate it—with a one-piece take-away. My hands, arms and shoulders all move the club away from the ball together. As you can see in the combined action photo above, this unified movement creates the wide swing arc previously visualized.

As you look at the photo, can you detect any lower body motion? Have my hips started to move with my shoulders? No, they remained in position because, at this phase of the swing, the lower body serves as a firm foundation.

The clubhead has a longer distance to travel than your hips, so it's natural for the upper body to start back first. The motion of the upper body, combined with the resistance of the lower body, also begins the process of storing power, which increases the farther back the shoulders turn. I'm really winding myself up like a spring that can release back to the ball once I reach the top.

KEEP THE TRIANGLE

A good mental image of the one-piece take-away is visualizing a triangle formed by both the arms and the chest. Maintain that visual throughout the swing. As you swing back, the club's grip is always in front of your chest.

All good golf swings look effortless, with outstanding timing and tempo. Staying connected limits various body parts from going off on their own and then making compensations to rejoin everything else at impact. Staying connected also makes timing the various swing elements on the downswing as easy as it looks.

1 As you begin the take-away, the triangle formed by the arms and chest moves together. Notice how the arrow from the grip is pointing to the chest. The key is maintaining this relationship throughout my swing.

2 The left arm is becoming parallel to the ground. The triangle has remained intact, with the grip still in front of Tom's chest. You'll lose accuracy and power if this relationship changes during any part of the swing.

Hips are just starting to rotate back, but you want to limit this movement to build torque.

3 Another key to a good backswing begins to show in this swing position: the shoulders' ability to rotate under chin. The triangle remains intact, with the grip in front of the chest.

Slight additional hip rotation can be seen. Look at the wrinkles in the shirt, and watch them tighten in the next photos as wind-up begins, the torque storing the power.

4 The triangle flexes a little but the unit remains intact to the top of the backswing. The arrow drawn from the grip indicates it remains correctly in front of the chest.

Can you see how the shoulders are rotating under the chin? Setting up at address with your chin out allows this to occur and prevents the shoulders from bumping the head, causing the swing to go off plane. Notice the shirt wrinkles tightening.

5 At the top of the backswing, everything is fully wound up and ready to release the power. Compare the full shoulder rotation with the limited hip position. Your mirror at home can help you duplicate the power being built here. Make a full and unified shoulder turn, restrict your hip rotation and check the wrinkles of your shirt for stored-up power.

B

TOE IN THE AIR

Tom feels the toe of his club is pointing to the sky during his backswing.

The peculiarity of a golf swing is that very often you feel you are doing something a certain way, but when you see it on video it's not quite that way. In my case, I want to feel the toe of my club in the air when my arms get waist high, when actually it's slightly closed. When I refer to getting the toe in the air, that would be the ultimate position.

I grew up with a shut face, so when I feel it's slightly open, in essence it's still slightly closed. But that's OK. In fact, when I have the slightly closed feeling, I play my best. When I'm playing poorly, the face is very closed. Conversely, some players are the opposite and get more laid off (open) when they play their best.

BACK TO THE TARGET

As I'm reaching the top of my backswing, I want the feeling that my back is facing the target. This indicates I will be fully wound up and ready to release all the power I've stored on the backswing.

Tom's lower body has moved very little in relation to his upper body. While the hips have remained almost parallel to the target line, his shoulders have rotated 90-degrees. That's why his back can now face the target.

GRIP POINTS INSIDE OF BALL

From the horizontal arm position I demonstrated, when I felt the toe of my club pointing in the air, all you have to do is swing straight up, as fellow TOUR player Scott Hoch shows in the photo below. The line from the grip of his club points to just inside the ball, verifying an excellent swing plane.

GRIP POINTS INSIDE THE BALL

At this position of the backswing, Scott Hoch's grip is pointing inside of the ball.

FLAT OR STEEP SWING PROBLEMS

Misunderstanding the arc on the backswing primarily causes the flat swing plane. The club must be swung back and up, not back and around. If your grip is pointing outside the ball, try to create a gap between your elbow and your side during the backswing. Check Tom's backswing photos to correct the problem.

The steep swing plane is usually caused by trying to control the clubhead, instead of allowing it to swing along on a natural arc. A descending blow along a steep downward swing plane is not the wide swing arc I want you to visualize.

With a flat swing plane, the grip points outside.

With a steep swing, the grip points inside the feet.

CORRECT BACKSWING IMAGE

The early-morning dew falling off Scott Hoch's club as he reaches the top of his backswing illustrates the perfect mental image of the backswing arc.

The water droplets draw the curved line of the continuous smooth motion as Scott's backswing goes up and around.

Smooth, effortless swings are simpler and more productive than trying to regain control of various body parts. Visualize this photo when you practice your swing.

B

BALLS

Arnold Palmer says the biggest difference in golf over the past 20 years is the way the golf ball has changed. When he joined the PGA TOUR, pros sometimes got golf balls that weren't always round! During the manufacturing and shipping processes, the rubber bands (an integral part of a ball's inner construction) shifted, causing them to be less than round. Sometimes they looked more like hard-boiled eggs.

Balls used to be tested before a pro would put them in the bag. It was a pretty simple test that required spinning the balls in a salt solution to check the buoyancy. The top of the ball would be marked, and then the ball would once again be spun in the solution. If the mark came up to the top, the ball was indeed round and could be played. On average, four to six balls out of a dozen ended up in the reject pile.

BALL COMPRESSION

At impact, Steve Pate's ball *(see left photo)* stayed on the clubface for only a fraction of a second, but all the energy was transferred in that brief time. His clubhead speed compressed the ball and powerfully launched it.

You can choose the amount of compression that is best suited for your game. Do you need a 100-compression ball? I don't use one! I play a 90-compression version.

I look for consistency in a golf ball. One of the ways to get consistent trajectory, spin and distance is to use a ball you can compress the same way every time. Remember—you must use the same ball for both driving and the short game.

An especially good swing may compress the harder 100-compression ball, and it may go an extra 10 yards when I don't want it to. I want a ball that reacts consistently, and the 90-compression ball has a softer cover, providing a soft feel as it comes off the clubface. This boosts my confidence, because I know I can make it do the same thing every time, especially when I need to spin it to create the perfect trajectory for a specific shot.

Clubhead speed compresses the ball and launches it powerfully.

HISTORICAL HIGHLIGHT

The first golf balls, called "feathery," were made out of feathers and cost about three times as much as a golf club. Only three could be turned out a day.

BALL POSITION

How do you know where your ball should be positioned for each club in your bag? Tom Lehman believes in keeping it simple, and illustrates his point with five colored balls. Follow the yellow ball as he shows the two ball positions he prefers.

The ball positions for your woods and most irons are presented here. For detailed information on ball positions for wedges, chipping, pitching and putting, please refer to those sections of the book.

BALL POSITION: DRIVER

For driving, the ideal ball position is the bottom of your swing arc. This might vary from person to person, but for consistent drives you need to find that point in your swing where the clubhead is moving parallel to the ground. This is the low point of your swing, allowing the driver to sweep through the ball.

At this point—assuming that you addressed the ball correctly—the clubhead impacts the ball square (90 degrees) to the target line. If you combine having the correct ball position with good posture, you should hit solid drives every time.

The yellow ball represents the position Tom located as the bottom of his swing arc for driving. Compare this position (which allows him to sweep through the ball) with the ball position for his irons (that encourages a descending blow).

BALL POSITION: IRONS

Irons need more of a descending blow, instead of the wood's sweeping action. This is still the bottom of my swing arc. The shorter club reaches the bottom of the swing arc farther back in my stance.

The iron returns to the 90-degree, square-to-the-target line that I set up correctly at address. The ball starts off along the target line. Vary your ball position on the range as you practice, and notice the direction of your shots. The correct ball position will quickly be revealed.

MARTIN'S FOOLPROOF LOCATING SYSTEM

A ball position slightly back of the bottom of the swing arc will result in a slightly open clubface at impact, while a position slightly forward results in a closed clubface. Both incorrect ball positions translate into off-line tee shots.

Here's my foolproof method for always knowing the exact position of the bottom of your swing arc for woods, regardless of the width of your stance: Line up the teed ball with your left shoulder joint (right shoulder joint for left-handers).

Regardless if you have a wide stance or a narrow one, always place the ball off your left shoulder joint. This will be the bottom of your swing when you are driving the ball or hitting fairway woods.

Using the same five balls as in the driver ball position photo above, Tom plays his irons two balls back from the driver position. Now the yellow ball is farther back in his stance.

B

BALL SPIN

Golf balls rotate as they fly through the air. The amount of this rotation, or spin, directly affects the trajectory and how the ball reacts after landing. The three types of spin are backspin, topspin and sidespin.

Sidespin results when the clubface is open or closed at impact.

Slices that bend uncontrollably from left to right are the result of left-to-right sidespin applied at impact with an open clubface slicing across the ball along an outside-to-in swing path.

Hooks that bend uncontrollably to the left develop because a closed clubface created severe right-to-left sidespin as it impacted the ball along an inside-to-out swing path.

Throughout the book, Tom Lehman demonstrates how to create sidespin for a variety of shots, but in this section Martin Hall discusses the subject of backspin.

BACKSPIN

Creating the degree of ball spin you need for a shot is one of the ways to dramatically improve your scoring-zone game. Good players have the feeling of cutting across and underneath the ball when they want to apply more ball spin. This requires additional wrist action.

On the other hand, if you want to limit the amount of spin, less wrist action is needed. I'll demonstrate both methods along with some helpful drills.

Let's begin with a simple illustration, using a tennis ball and ping-pong paddle, showing what causes the ball to spin.

Using a tennis ball and ping-pong paddle, Martin Hall demonstrates how to add or limit the amount of backspin in this section.

CUTTING UNDERNEATH THE BALL

If you've ever played tennis or other racket sports, you'll recognize the feeling of cutting across the ball when you hit a slice spin shot, as the photo below shows.

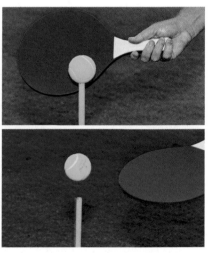

The swing is cutting across and under the tennis ball. As the paddle cuts underneath, the ball immediately starts to climb. This is the same feeling you want when creating additional backspin for your golf shots.

CREATING BACKSPIN

Hitting down on the back of the ball is the way to hit a weak shot with backspin. Why would you want additional backspin? My feeling is you wouldn't for most shots. I think the best short-game players in the world try not to spin the ball. But there are times you might need to.

A good example is a downwind par-3 with hard greens, and you must stop the ball quickly. I'll demonstrate how to play the shot using a 7-iron off the tee.

The checklist should help you create backspin.

THE SWING FOR CREATING BACKSPIN

1 Set up more behind the ball. You should be aware of looking at the back of the ball at this point.

2 Stay behind the ball and swing the clubhead up in the air as fast as you can. This does not mean your backswing is overly fast. Rather, it refers to the clubhead's vertical height. A little more folding in the elbows will help accomplish this.

3 As you reach the top of your backswing, get the feeling of throwing the clubhead a little more from the top, something slicers unfortunately do regularly.

4 The downswing begins to show the wrists uncocking earlier in the swing than normal. Wristy swings add more ball spin.

5 In this wristy downswing, the clubhead is passing the hands very quickly on its way to cutting under the ball.

6 Past impact, the wrists have released. This is a much narrower swing than normal, with a much earlier wrist release.

7 A complete follow-through allows you to continue the swing speed to the end. Any abbreviated finish would inhibit the wrist release that is needed to add more backspin.

B

LIMITING BACKSPIN

The way to limit the amount of backspin on the ball is to play a shot almost opposite to the one that creates additional backspin. More wrist action was needed to create backspin, so less wrist action limits it.

With less rotation on the ball, it will not climb as much. If you have a shot into the wind, for example, the ball needs to bore through it. The harder you hit the shot, the more backspin is applied, and you will come up short.

The checklist should help you limit backspin.

THE SWING

STAND CLOSER

Place a club on your heels (top photo) for your normal stance, to illustrate how much closer you need to move to the ball when playing a backspin-limiting shot (bottom photo and inset).

LIMIT WRIST ACTION

PARTIAL BACKSWING

The advantage of taking more club (a 6-iron instead of a 9-iron) is that you do not have to swing as hard, which causes the ball to bore instead of climb. Allow your arms to dominate this partial backswing.

IMPACT

The key to limiting backspin is to not cut under the ball with a wristy swing. Here at impact you can see how firm the wrists are to prevent that from occurring. As a result, there's no additional clubface loft or cutting action.

FOLLOW-THROUGH

The wrists remain unbroken even at this abbreviated finish position. Don't make a complete around-the-back follow-through when you want to limit backspin.

BELLY WEDGE

When your ball rests up against the higher collar of the second cut of rough around the green, shot selection is critical if you want to get the ball close to the pin. Chipping through the taller grass traps too much material between the clubface and the ball, and distance control becomes a guessing game.

Instead of a normal chip shot, use your sand wedge and skim across the top of the rough, impacting the ball at its middle—the belly.

GLIDE ON THE GRASS

Hitting the ball right in its belly becomes easier once you learn to use the higher grass as a guide. Gliding the clubhead back and forward on this grass brings the face directly into the ball's belly.

LEVEL FOLLOW-THROUGH

Notice the ball is only slightly airborne as it carries over the fringe and onto the green. Gliding across the grass on the forward swing and keeping the clubhead level on the follow-through prevented a descending swing path. As a result, shot control was maintained as impact was made at the belly of the ball.

B

BUMP AND RUN

The bump and run shot is overlooked as a potent weapon in today's three-wedge world. Picking a target in front of the green, landing the ball close to or on the green, and then having it run the rest of the way to the pin is a higher percentage shot for many golfers to play.

The key, as with all shots, is to first visualize the shot and then have the skills to hit it. Tom Lehman helps you with both below.

Bump and run shots are just that—they land and then run. For that to occur, the trajectory must not be too high (the ball will have limited running ability after landing) or too low (it will land hot and run right through the green). Pin placement and how much green you have to work with dictate club selection. Remember:

Tom's bump and run shot will land in front of the green and roll the rest of the way to the pin.

- More clubhead loft = higher trajectories = less release and roll.

- Less clubhead loft = lower trajectories = more release and roll.

In the photo at left, I have a considerable amount of green to work with and want the ball to land and roll a long distance. My choice is a less-lofted club—a 9-iron instead of a wedge.

IMPACT IS THE KEY POSITION

Because the ball must run after landing, you must tailor the shot to encourage that type of release. The impact position is vital to success.

1 Notice how Tom's hands are ahead of the clubface at impact, de-lofting the club.

2 The ball will fly to the green along a lower trajectory.

3 The flight distance is to the landing spot, not the pin, so pick a target that allows plenty of room for the ball to roll.

BURIED LIES

Whenever the ball plugs or gets buried in a bunker, the problem is getting enough club under the ball to dislodge it from the sand. Chi Chi Rodriguez shows the results of his up-and-down efforts at right, while David Frost (below) chops up and then brings his arm behind his back on the follow-through.

Chi Chi solves buried lies (inset) by picking the club straight up in the air and then coming straight down.

CHOP UP

David's backswing is an almost straight-up motion. This is a vertical motion that is solely designed to get the club in the best position to come straight down and through the ball.

LEFT ARM BEHIND BACK

While his left arm does not actually go behind his back, David Frost feels as if it gets sucked there. When faced with a buried lie, rehearse this motion before stepping in to play the shot. Always program your brain and muscle memory for shots that require special techniques to succeed.

B

CENTRIFUGAL FORCE

Centrifugal force creates the downswing's half second of incredible clubhead speed.

CLUBHEAD SPEED

Turn your swing over to the powers of centrifugal force and clubhead speed increases dramatically. Trying to swing fast can't generate the same clubhead speed as allowing the laws of physics to propel the club. This whirling motion propels the clubhead around a wide arc that is uninterrupted by physical or mental roadblocks.

If you ever played *crack the whip* when you were younger, or watched the chorus line of an ice show skate around a fixed-axis circle adding one skater at a time, these are examples of centrifugal force at work. Centrifugal force generates the greatest speed the farther out from the center you are, so the outside skater is propelled the fastest just as your extended clubhead rotates faster than your body does during a golf swing. After a primer on how centrifugal force is created (page 41), Martin Hall hands you a broom to help you develop your centrifugal force.

LITTLE CIRCLE/BIG CIRCLE

Five foot-10, 165-pound Scott McCarron consistently drives the ball over 285 yards. His 120-mph clubhead speed, created by centrifugal force, is the reason. McCarron allows this process to occur naturally by "trusting my swing." Also, he does not make any midcourse corrections during his downswing that would interrupt clubhead speed. His body is the *little circle* while his clubhead follows the *big circle.*

✔CHECKLIST
DEVELOPING UNINTERRUPTED CENTRIFUGAL FORCE

✔ Set up address position with correct posture and angles.

✔ Grip pressure is light enough to feel the clubhead.

✔ Backswing positions the club correctly at the top.

✔ Backswing weight is loaded up on the side of the body *away* from the target.

✔ Transition through impact is a free-flowing, accelerating process around a fixed spine angle. There are no midcourse swing plane changes.

PGA TOUR pro Scott McCarron demonstrates the two-circle centrifugal force process. As he rotates his wrist in a small circle, his car keys, attached to a rope, are whirling around the big circle at a higher rate of speed than his wrist. The keys weigh more than the string, just as the clubhead weighs more than the shaft.

TOM'S SHOTMAKING TIPS

FREE-FLOWING CENTRIFUGAL FORCE

With a fixed spine angle serving as the axis for your swing circle, your smaller, connected body rotation propels the extended (out from the body) clubhead along a circle of wider diameter. Physics propels the clubhead at a greater rate of speed than the slower-rotating body.

A tension-free grip allows the clubhead to naturally set the angles of your wrists during the backswing, and release them during the follow-through. This increases clubhead speed.

C

MARTIN SWINGS THE BROOM

Swinging a simple household broom can be the centrifugal force training link for developing increased power and distance. Its weight keeps you linked together to move it while the weight of the straw helps develop a sense of *feeling your clubhead.*

1- ADDRESS

Nothing fancy about this broom, but it's pure magic when used to improve your swing. Simulate setting up to a target, making sure your grip and posture are correct.

2- BACKSWING AND TRANSITION

Rotate to the top of your backswing, feeling the weight of the straw, and continue back as your hips and knees begin the transition toward the target. Feel how your lower body must provide the leverage and generate the power to get the broomstick shaft moving from the top down and around toward the ball.

3- PAST IMPACT EXTENSION

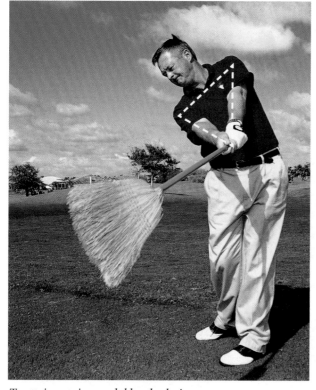

To attain maximum clubhead velocity, you want your clubhead extended out like this broom head during your swing. Notice how the power triangle stays linked, keeping the grip in front of the chest, as the broom fully extends past impact.

The broom head has swung around a wide swing arc. Power comes from smaller body rotation. Little circle/big circle has generated powerful broom head centrifugal force.

4- FOLLOW-THROUGH

The whirling broom head comes to a stop and you should finish facing the simulated target. The swing was free flowing and powerful.

TOM SAYS:

You don't always have to go to the practice range to keep your game sharp. Muscle memory can be maintained at high levels at home using the drills in this book.

Then when you do get to the practice range, your basic fundamentals for good golf will be second nature, allowing total concentration on the vital aspect of the game: hitting your targets.

CHIPPING

"Chipping is the easiest way for the average golfer to shave strokes from his or her score. Becoming good around the green is essential." —Tom Lehman

Do you squander strokes around the green, occasionally getting it close but sometimes winding up in a different zip code? Take Tom's statement seriously. It is possible to save a minimum of five strokes each round once you consistently chip the ball close to the pin or, even better, hole the chip.

Chip shots follow a putting line to the hole, since they roll most of the way. Chip the ball accurately on that line with the correct speed, and you should be flirting with the cup on a regular basis. Tom provides his professional insights and tips here, then Martin Hall demonstrates his teaching drills.

With Scottsdale's famed Pinnacle Peak in the background, Tom Lehman chips off the fringe.

CHIPPING: TECHNIQUE

✔ CHECKLIST
ACCURATE CHIPPING

✔ Find the putting line to the hole.

✔ Select the proper club for the distance and choke down on the grip.

✔ Lower body must remain quiet, so open your stance to pre-set the space for your arms to swing through.

✔ Descending blow is the angle of attack.

✔ Play the ball back in your stance with the hands forward.

✔ A rhythmical swing encourages solid contact with a sense of feel.

QUIET LOWER BODY

As far as your lower body is concerned, chipping is like putting. In both situations your lower body must remain quiet to achieve accuracy. Solid contact with the ball is vital, and any motion that slightly moves your body position negatively affects your results.

The action photo below clearly illustrates the different roles of my upper and lower body. Resting on a solid foundation, my shoulders and arms have all the motion responsibility, swinging the club away and then back down and through the ball.

Tom's lower body stays quiet when he chips.

CHOKE DOWN ON THE CLUB

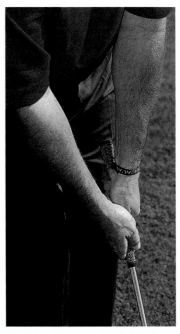

Choking down on the club is the first order of business when addressing the ball for a chip. This encourages an improved sense of feel with your hands.

C

OPEN STANCE

Maintain a quiet lower body for accuracy. During a full swing the hips rotate open prior to impact, providing room for the hands and arms to swing the club through on plane. But for chipping, open your stance to pre-set that space so you can keep your lower body still. Less lower body movement means better accuracy.

SOLID CONTACT SETUP

Solid contact is the goal. To encourage that result, play the ball back in your stance. One more step also helps: Pre-set your hands ahead of the ball.

TOM'S SHOTMAKING TIPS

GREEN FIRMNESS

It's much easier to chip on a firm green than a soft one because you don't know how much the ball landing on a soft spot will check up on you. With a firm green you know the ball will release and roll.

My idea of chipping is to find a way to judge the bounce and spin so in the end I can anticipate how much release to expect once the ball lands. Knowing what the ball is going to do after it hits, and matching a technique to that situation, is what makes you a good chipper.

RHYTHMICAL SWING

With light grip pressure I want to swing the club back, descend down and through the ball, then follow through to an almost mirror position of my backswing. This is the definition of my rhythmical chipping swing.

QUIET LOWER BODY

Keeping your lower body quiet, the shoulders and arms swing the club back. Drawing an imaginary line in your mind, can you visualize the club's descending path back to the ball?

SOLID HIT

Solid doesn't mean powerful. You should hit all ball, not the grass before the ball. Impact with the grass prior to the ball scrubs off some of the clubhead speed that was essential to get the ball rolling to the cup. A descending clubhead path reduces the chance of that happening, and the ball is hit with the loft you set at address.

SOLID WRISTS

Do not break your wrists when you chip. Keep your wrists firm past impact. This sends the ball off on a flatter trajectory. Breaking the wrists adds another factor that negatively affects your feel for the shot. You judged the amount of speed the ball needs to get to the hole, and your sense of feel dictates how fast to swing the clubhead.

But if you have to factor in the wrists breaking or the club impacting the ground, even today's most sophisticated computer could not solve that equation. Keep everything simple by limiting your moving parts.

CLUB SELECTION

My chipping preference is to land the ball on the green and get it rolling as quickly as possible. Because it's hard to judge feel if the ball is spinning too much, I use less lofted clubs for chipping, maybe even a 6-iron for longer chips.

PRACTICE THE DESCENDING HIT

A good way to develop a feel for the descending angle of attack is to use a club on the ground to regulate the path.

- Place a club on the ground on line with your back foot.

- Play the ball off your right toe.

- Make a short backstroke and skim over the shaft to find the perfect downswing angle to the back of the ball.

DRILL

MARTIN'S ACCURACY DRILL

Even for a chip shot your club must follow a swing arc. A common mistake—and one this drill helps you avoid—is thinking that to be accurate you must swing the club out straight past impact along the target line to the hole. This is incorrect.

The club must follow its arc, even the short one that chipping requires. To train yourself to follow the correct path, instead of finishing straight out, try this drill.

FOLLOW THE ARC

Place a club on the ground to simulate the target line to the hole (left). Continue on the swing arc past impact (right) so that your club finishes on the inside. Your wrists should be flat and unbroken.

C

CHIPPING: DISTANCE CONTROL

As you chip, your ball should stay in the air just long enough to carry over the fringe before landing on the green. But all the pins you encounter are not the same distance away. Some are close and others aren't.

Players on the PGA TOUR, for the most part, believe accuracy is attained by rolling the ball instead of lofting it. The swing and landing spot are the same, but one element is changed—club selection.

Billy Mayfair tries to limit the variables and goes to three clubs to take care of the distance. They work for him, but you should audition three clubs of your own. Below are Billy's choices.

PGA TOUR professional Billy Mayfair has three "go to" clubs he counts on for distance control.

PIN	BILLY'S CHOICE
Close pins	**Sand wedge**
Middle pins	**9-iron**
Far pins	**7-iron**

TOM'S SHOTMAKING TIPS

CLUB SELECTION

Billy Mayfair feels that practicing with a few clubs instills confidence and provides feedback to make the adjustments needed for the various pin placements. Choose three clubs you prefer and experiment with ball position to make them even more versatile for any situation that might arise.

CLUB DISTANCES

When SENIOR PGA TOUR professional Isao Aoki asks his caddie the yardage for a shot, he can pick the exact club to match it. Knowing how far you hit your clubs is important, but you better be hitting your shots in the center of the clubface for that to be a consistent number.

"Hitting the ball consistently in the middle of the clubface is the only way for determining consistent yardages for each club." *—Martin Hall*

Here's a fact of golf life: If you hit the ball just ½ inch off the center of the clubface, you will be giving up roughly 10 or 15 yards in accuracy. Any movement away from the center of the face's sweetspot costs you yardage as well.

So how can you really determine your club distances? Martin Hall provides some advice in this section, and we sprinkle a few shotmaking tips from Tom to help.

This temporary decal, available at golf specialty stores, shows the ball print of a sweetspot hit.

AVERAGE DISTANCES
IN YARDS

Club	Beginner	Average	Excellent*
Driver	190	220	250-285
2-wood	180	215	235-275
3-wood	170	210	225-250
4-wood	165	205	215-225
5-wood	150	195	200-215
2-iron	145	180	190-210
3-iron	135	170	180-190
4-iron	125	160	170-180
5-iron	120	155	165-175
6-iron	115	145	160-170
7-iron	105	140	150-165
8-iron	95	130	140-155
9-iron	80	115	125-135
P-wedge	70	100	110-125
S-wedge	55	80	95-110
L-wedge	short distance with high trajectory		

*Excellent includes low handicap amateurs and professional golfers

C

CONSISTENT CLUB DISTANCES

SQUARE CLUBFACE

Consistent distances are the result of several factors, including a square clubface and sweetspot hits.

This face is square to the target line. Repeating this position at impact sends the ball along the target line without the sidespin that can rob both distance and accuracy.

- *Open face at impact = slice spin.*

- *Closed face at impact = hook spin.*

TOM'S SHOTMAKING TIPS

ACCURATE CLUB YARDAGE

Knowing how far you hit your clubs helps one other aspect of your game—confidence. Totally committing to a shot produces the best results, but unless you really know your club's yardage you subconsciously adjust for the unknown.

For example, many higher handicap golfers play for the yardage they may have hit the club one or two times in the past. Good golf scores do not know which club you hit, but they do reflect a series of good choices.

So test yourself for accurate club yardage now and continue testing as you improve your game. Then, when you commit to a shot like a pro, you really will be committing to the shot.

ARE YOU HITTING THE SWEETSPOT?

You can achieve consistent club distances only if you hit the ball on the sweetspot. Apply decals or powder paint (available through golf specialty stores) to your clubface to help you see how close to the sweetspot you're hitting the ball. Here are three examples.

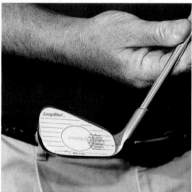

Martin Hall shows off his sweetspot hit.

SWEETSPOT HIT

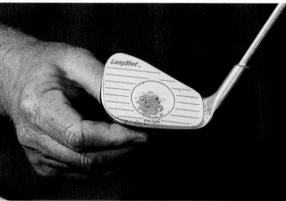

This ball impacted the face in the middle of the sweetspot. If this is your report card, you have graduated to accurate yardage assignments for each club.

HEEL HIT

If you see this heel hit on your clubface, your shot patterns are usually to the left or a shank to the right or left. Heel hits close the clubface down at impact. Hitting the ball on the heel can be a result of:

- *Standing too close to the ball at address.*

- *Swinging inside to out.*

TOE HIT

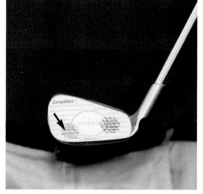

Here the same decal shows the difference between the previously mentioned heel hit and a toe hit (arrow). Hitting it on the toe opens the clubface, usually sending the ball to the right. The reasons can include:

- *Standing too far away from the ball at address.*

- *Swinging outside to in.*

Making
Shots

48

SWEETSPOT SHADOW DRILL

Use an old shaft and a sunny day to work on your sweetspot technique. One reason for inconsistently hitting the sweetspot is not having the bottom of your swing arc in a constant position. Vary that position and you vary the clubface relationship to the target line. This drill helps correct that problem and is a major step toward assigning meaningful accurate yardages to your clubs.

1. CAST THE SHADOW

Place an old shaft or pole in the ground, with the sun angle behind it, to cast a shadow in your direction.

2. AIM FOR THE BACK

Line up several balls so their back is resting on the shadow line. You want your clubhead at this square position at impact.

3. HIT THE BACK

Work your way down the line. This trains you to improve your sweetspot accuracy by hitting each ball right in the back and at the correct bottom of your swing arc.

Change your body's position to the ball, either forward or backward slightly, to compare shot pattern results. The straight hits are sweetspot hits!

C

CLUBFACE ANGLE MODIFICATIONS

HOODED CLUBFACE

Hooding the clubface means to close it at address so that it's not pointing directly at your target. This will result in a lower shot to the left that can sometimes be beneficial to steer around trouble. Usually you need to aim more to the right to compensate for the ball flight direction.

Former British Open champion Ian Baker-Finch is hitting a hooded shot to avoid a rock directly in his swing path. The ball is flying on the desired path to the green.

OPEN CLUBFACE

In this simulated impact position, the clubface returns to its open-at-address position in the bunker. Utilized to create additional height for specific clubs, it is important to open the face before gripping to allow a natural return to this position.

TOM'S SHOTMAKING TIPS

SWING PLANE FOR MODIFIED ANGLES

You can make a single club do the work of several just by opening or closing the face. Two important shotmaking tips to remember are:

1 Always make your clubface modification prior to gripping the club.

2 Your swing should follow the line of your feet. Do not swing in the direction the clubface has been adjusted.

CONCENTRATION

Tom Lehman knows how important maintaining concentration is for PGA TOUR professionals.

On the PGA TOUR a fan may see a player pull his club, walk behind the ball and then someone makes a noise or moves, causing a disruption of his thought process. They wonder why he might give the offender an unfriendly look as he puts the club back in his bag.

Unfortunately some people don't understand that every movement a TOUR player makes after pulling a club is part of their established pre-shot routine, and the routine is a source of confidence. With many players out on TOUR, once the routine is broken the process has to be started all over again.

If you hear a TOUR player talk to a marshal about the sign he's holding, the player is only trying to make sure his routine isn't broken by the wonderful ladies and gentlemen who volunteer their time and are the backbone of any golf tournament. There couldn't be a tournament without them. But a marshal who puts their "Quiet Please" sign up late can also break a player's concentration, which again means the process has to start all over again.

TOM SAYS:

It isn't that we're prima donnas, it's that golf is essentially a mind game. Unlike most other sports, the ball is not going to move until we hit it. We don't react to the ball; we have to mentally prepare to manipulate the ball a certain way for a given situation. This takes concentration and the confidence of pre-programming the mind with familiar feels and thoughts.

Lee Trevino's concentration extends to his finish. Even to the jovial Trevino, concentration is an important part of his game.

JACK NICKLAUS'S CONCENTRATION ROUTINE

Jack Nicklaus was and still is an intense competitor. Early in his career he learned how to concentrate effectively by limiting it only to the times when he was preparing for a shot.

As he walked to the next shot he would allow himself to relax and look around at the surroundings. But when he reached his ball or prepared to tee off, the intense concentration returned.

C

CONNECTED SWING

All through this book you will find numerous references to the connected swing, power triangle and one-piece take-away. They all have one thing in common: efficiency. When you walk or jog, your various body parts are not going off in every direction. Instead, each stays interconnected so that bending and weight transfer occurs efficiently.

Why should the highly refined golf swing be any different? Staying connected is the efficient way to control the timing of the various elements of the swing into a harmonious result—an on-line, accurate and powerful impact. Martin Hall demonstrates some drills to keep you connected throughout your swing.

Tom's swing is connected and efficient. Martin Hall's drills will help your swing get—and stay—that way.

DRILL

MEDICINE BALL DRILL

This drill connects your hands, arms and body, putting you in sync while strengthening the mid-body muscles.

1 Hold the medicine ball in the center of a good address position. Be sure to retain the spine angle set at address throughout this drill to maximize its effect.

2 Swing back so that your arms become horizontal to the ground. Your chest, arms and hands must stay connected in a triangle to efficiently swing the heavy ball back.

3 With hips leading the way, the power triangle stays connected as the ball enters the impact zone.

4 The ball was tossed at the point past impact where the club would be at full extension thanks to centrifugal force. Staying connected all the way through your swing is the only way you can improve your power and accuracy.

TRIANGLE CONNECTION DRILL

The noted instructor Jimmy Ballard believes everything must stay together during the swing. The club must never get outside the triangle and the grip should always be in front of the chest. Try this proven Ballard drill to keep your wrists, hands, arms and chest moving together in sync.

This drill can be done several ways, but Jimmy Ballard says that you should place the club's butt on your chest and hold it with your arms outstretched, as shown. The triangular relationship formed is very obvious and it must be maintained throughout your swing.

As you make little swings, keep the same position and the triangle remains intact. Another time to use this drill is while you're waiting for your turn to hit. It programs the mind for a connected golf swing.

C

DIFFICULT CHIPS

For most chip shots your lie is just off the green, requiring only basic technique to get the ball in or close to the hole. But on occasion you may find yourself in some unusual situations where a poorly played chip costs you strokes. To avoid this, adapt your thought process, along with your technique, to match the situation.

Three examples are shown in this section—putting, downhill and multi-breaking chips—and Martin Hall guides you through them all.

Tom Lehman practices chipping to different pins, adjusting his technique to match each situation.

PUTTING CHIP

Sometimes you'll find your ball in a snagly lie around the green. You need to make adaptations to limit the amount of clubface exposed to potential entanglement with the grass. The technique at right puts a wedge up on its toe and, combined with a putting-type stroke, lets you play this shot successfully.

Hitting the ball off a wedge's toe prevents a club from getting caught in snagly grass.

✔ CHECKLIST
PUTTING CHIPS

✔ Pick out your putting line to the hole.

✔ Position a wedge's shaft more vertically so the clubhead rests on its toe.

✔ Place the grip end of your club against the inside of your left arm (right arm for left-handers).

✔ Use your normal putting grip.

✔ Keep the shaft pressed against your arm and make an arm-dominated swing back and through, so that you impact the ball on the club's toe.

TOM'S SHOTMAKING TIPS

OPEN STANCE

When you chip the ball, accuracy is vital. Limiting as many moving body parts as possible enhances accuracy, because there is less chance of something throwing off your swing plane, preventing the clean impact you need.

Opening your stance—but aiming the club to the target—pre-sets the room needed for your arms to swing the club through. Then you don't need to rotate your hips during the swing to get them out of the way. This quiet lower body, with its open stance, lets the arms and club stay on plane so your ball can stay on target.

ADDRESS

Standing as near to the ball as you would for a putt brings the shaft to a more vertical position, setting the wedge on its toe. Notice the ball is positioned just off Martin's toe.

SHAFT ON FOREARM

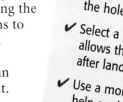

Choke down on the club, because standing closer creates a vertical shaft and the club becomes longer than normal. Rest the butt against the inside of your left forearm (right forearm for left-handers). Keep it pressed against the forearm throughout the swing, eliminating the chance for any wrist-breaking.

PUTTING GRIP

Grip your wedge just as you would your putter. Be sure the shaft is pressing on the inside of your forearm.

ON THE TOE

The changes shown here have placed the wedge on its toe. Maintaining a firm wrist position and an extremely quiet lower body through a short stroke is the next step.

POP THE BALL

This action photo shows the ball popping out of the snagly grass, thanks to adaptations from a normal chipping technique. Notice how quiet the lower body remains during the stroke, leading to a clean and firm impact.

DOWNHILL CHIPS

The speed of a ball rolling downhill is something you need to control for downhill chips. Understanding the modifications to your normal chipping technique can easily do that.

ADJUST THE SETUP

Bruce Fleisher plays his downhill chips by:

* *Finding the putting line to the hole and a landing target on that line.*

* *Using a wedge.*

* *Positioning the ball back in his stance.*

✔**CHECKLIST**
DOWNHILL CHIPS

✔ Pick out the putting line to the hole.

✔ Select a landing target that allows the ball room to run after landing.

✔ Use a more lofted club to help apply the brakes after landing.

✔ Play the ball back in your stance.

✔ Hit down and through the ball to let the clubhead loft apply some backspin.

LANDING

Bruce chips to his landing target. Hitting down and through the ball with the wedge creates extra backspin to apply the brakes after the ball lands. Gravity then takes over, feeding the ball to the pin.

D

MULTI-BREAKING CHIP

Occasionally you find yourself chipping to a green that is contoured, and your putting line encounters several breaks on the way to the hole. Chipping to the target line is important, but you have to consider distance and the speed as well.

VISUALIZE THE LINE

Billy Mayfair is facing a long downhill chip with several breaks. First step: Find the line and select a target on the first part of that line.

SETUP

Billy selects a 7-iron and positions the ball back in his stance. He chokes down on the grip and moves his hands forward to set the correct club angle.

IMPACT

Chipping down with a descending angle quickly pops the ball into the air along the line to the hole. Do not break your wrists; keep them flat through impact.

TOM'S SHOTMAKING TIPS

FEEL

Feel is not something anyone can teach you. It only comes from practice and repetition. You can encourage feel by relaxing, gripping the club lightly and swinging rhythmically.

Tennis players feel they play their best when they *feel the ball staying on the strings* as long as possible. Golfers play their best when they *feel the ball staying on their clubface* as long as possible.

• Adjust the tempo of your swing to develop this feeling first.

• Adjust your feel for distance by keeping this tempo and adjusting the length of your backswing and follow-through to match the situation.

DIFFICULT PITCHES

Pitch shots must fly in the air higher and longer than chip shots (for more information see Pitch Shots). You will frequently face situations where the lie is not exactly level. In fact, it can be very uneven, and when a hazard lies between your ball and the green, it helps to know how to adjust. Tom Lehman and Martin Hall deal with several different lies here.

Tom lofts the ball high off a downhill lie. This is definitely a difficult pitch.

DOWNHILL LIE PITCH

Downhill lies produce shots that go lower than normal. Change your normal pitching technique to match the shot.

✔CHECKLIST
DOWNHILL PITCH

✔ Select a more lofted club.

✔ Keep weight on downhill foot.

✔ Hit down the slope.

✔ Finish high.

✔ Allow the ball an adequate running distance after landing.

SETUP

Tom uses a wedge to provide additional loft for this downhill shot. The stance is open with the legs farther apart than normal, allowing ample room for the arms to swing the club through on-plane. Weight is balanced on the downhill leg to maintain stability throughout the entire swing.

BACKSWING

Backswing and downswing follow the slope. Notice how the arm dominates the swing as compared to a quiet lower body. Don't risk losing your balance, and consequently moving the bottom of the swing arc, to produce a poor effort.

IMPACT

The club is sliding through the grass along the slope line. As it slides under the ball, the wedge's loft will get it airborne quickly.

PAST IMPACT

Stay balanced on your downhill leg. Notice the ball is already approaching head height and will continue even higher, easily carrying over the bunker for a soft landing on the green.

HIGH, BALANCED FOLLOW-THROUGH

Finish high and in balance on your downhill leg. Accelerating through the ball provides the height and momentum needed to produce a quality golf shot.

D

UPHILL PITCH

An uphill pitch shot really requires a major adjustment in your technique: a rounded swing. Here, the ball is way above Martin's feet in the grass and he's standing in the bunker.

Martin Hall's adjustment for this uphill pitch shot is a rounded swing.

SETUP

Standing in the bunker with the ball considerably higher than your feet presents an interesting challenge. With the target line right of the camera view you can't stand high enough to create a downward attack angle. To adjust, hold the club at the bottom of the grip to shorten it, and aim 10 to 15 degrees right of the target. Maintain this same clubhead height at both ends of your swing in order to make clean contact with the ball.

ROUNDED BACKSWING

This action photo demonstrates the rounded swing arc as the club is taken away from the ball. The lower body remains extremely quiet, allowing arms and hands to take the club back.

ROUNDED SIDE SWING

Sounds like baseball terminology, but this is the only method to make clean contact, advancing the ball onto the green. Notice how steady the lower body is. Any movement changes the swing arc's relationship to the ball. Arms only please!

RESULTS

The ball leaves the clubhead with plenty of loft and energy to reach the green. The key to this swing is your tempo. Smooth swings accomplish greatness. Jerky swings produce high handicaps and frustration.

TOM'S SHOTMAKING TIPS

PATIENCE

Difficult shots require patience. Think it through, visualizing exactly what you want the ball to do. See it land and react so that targets and clubs can be properly selected.

Use your practice swing to rehearse the shot, establishing the feelings and swing plane needed to match the situation. Swings for every shot are not the same. Have the patience to program your mind for the shot you're facing.

SIDEHILL PITCHES

Sidehill pitches never end up where you aim, so the first adjustment is compensating for the hill you are playing. Next, you must stay on plane.

Martin Hall's sidehill pitch shot was aimed to the left to compensate for the ball's tendency to drift off target.

CHECKLIST
SIDEHILL PITCH

✔ Balls below your feet will drift to the right so aim more to the left.

✔ Balls above your feet will drift to the left so aim more to the right.

✔ Bend from the waist for shots below your feet.

✔ Stand up taller by narrowing your stance for balls that are above your feet.

✔ Keep your swing on plane for success.

SETUP

This lie is slightly below the feet. If compensation isn't made, the results will be poor. Bend slightly more from the waist than normal and adjust your aim slightly to the right.

BACKSWING

The club swings back on plane as a result of a one-piece take-away. Shoulders, arms and hands swing the club away. The lower body rotates slightly back. This action photo provides a good visual image of an on-plane swing.

DOWNSWING

The power triangle moves together down and into the ball. Notice how the grip stays positioned in front of the body. The left knee began the transition back to the ball, allowing the hips to clear enough room for the arms to swing the club through. If the hips block the arms, your shot will go way to the right.

THE RESULTS

A perfect pitch. The ball starts out to the left and will drift slightly to the right. This height allows it to settle softly on the green when it lands.

D

DISTANCE CONTROL

Smoothness is the key to distance control for your short game. Unlike the acceleration you want in your long game downswing, it is totally inappropriate for short game accuracy and distance control. Instead of accelerating, think in terms of matching your backswing length to your downswing length. Martin Hall demonstrates using a clockface as an example.

Tom Lehman regulates his distance by matching the length of his backswing and downswing.

Using my left arm to develop feel, I'm matching various backswings and downswings to develop additional distance. Always swing smoothly with a defined tempo instead of slow on the backswing and fast on the downswing.

9 TO 3: SHORT SHOTS

Short backswing and follow-through for close shots.

10 TO 2: MEDIUM SHOTS

Standard backswing and follow-through for medium-range shots.

11 TO 1: LONG SHOTS

Long backswing and follow-through for long shots.

DOWNSWING

Here are three outstanding examples of acceleration. All share the same basic idea: Stored-up fuel creates power.

1 The Space Shuttle leaving the launch pad

2 A dragster accelerating off the line with its wheels smoking

3 A PGA TOUR professional's downswing

The first two are easily understood, as engines create energy by burning fuel. But where is the commonality with a professional golfer's downswing? After all, solid fuel or liquid nitrogen doesn't propel Tom Lehman. Tom's fuel is his weight transfer, and that powers his swing just as efficiently as the other two examples.

Tom Lehman's rapidly accelerating downswing reaches the power slot position. Delaying the release—as a result of this highly desirable position—increases the amount of velocity the clubhead imparts on the ball at impact.

DOWNSWING EARLY STAGES

The acceleration of my downswing begins at the transition. As my left knee and left hip begin rotating toward the target, the shoulders continue back, increasing the wound-up energy. All my weight is on my side away from the target. The fuel tank is full.

In both photos (taken only a fraction of a second apart) the club does not look like it has moved much,

If you look closely and compare the shaft positions against the tree branches in the background, both photos show some club shaft motion. The shaft is more to the right as it drops to the inside, indicating acceleration back to the ball is about to be unleashed.

but the legs certainly have. The lower body can be easily seen rotating toward the ball. Less bend in the left knee (photo 2) shows the early transfer of weight over to the target side of my body.

D

POWER SLOT

The power triangle brings the club into the power slot. Increasing your distance and accuracy is the result, once you duplicate how I'm pulling the butt of the club down toward the ball. In these photos, notice the shaft swinging down from the inside, instead of a slicer's outside-the-line casting position. The grip portion stays in front of my chest. I'm linked, creating power. The clubhead is rapidly accelerating.

Look at the power slot created (1). The clubhead fully reaches the power slot (2) and the nomenclature is perfect for this position. The shaft is parallel to the ground, pointing toward the target and extending back, creating a wider swing arc. This extra width allows the clubhead to gain additional speed from centrifugal force's power prior to impact.

DOWNSWING WRIST AND HIP ANGLES

Maintaining your wrist angles is vital for a powerful downswing. Release them early and linkage is lost along with your power. Notice how my hips have rotated past their address position below, creating room for the power triangle to pull the rapidly accelerating club through the impact zone on plane.

APPROACHING THE POWER SLOT

Notice how Tom's right wrist retains the angle set at the top of the backswing (circled, inset photo) while his left wrist is flat. Lose this angle and you lose power.

PRE-IMPACT AND DELAYED HIT

The wrist angle remains important in these stages of the downswing. The big mistake is releasing your left wrist too early in the swing. Retain your angles as I do for longer drives.

Don't release your wrists too early; Tom hasn't (1). Notice how the hands and grip are in front of Tom's body (2) but the clubhead lags behind. This is the delayed hit that allows the clubhead to increase its speed just before impact. The equivalent is the extra bit of energy being wound up as the transition began, only in this case extra clubhead speed is being created by delaying the hit.

DIVOTS

You know what a divot is, but do you know what they can tell you about your swing? Tom Lehman sheds some new light on these missing chunks of earth.

I take divots but never steep ones. I want to see the top of the roots under the divot when the grass is gone. The divot can be long but it has to be shallow for me to know my swing was a good one.

Tom prefers a shallow divot that shows his sole came through level at impact.

You should be able to self-analyze yourself without being a pro to see what you may be doing wrong. Looking at your divots provides the clues.

✔CHECKLIST
INTERPRETING DIVOTS

✔ Look at your divot to understand what happened during your swing.

✔ Straight divots or a slight arc indicate a club arrived along the correct swing plane.

✔ Deep divots indicate your swing was steep, maybe too steep.

✔ Divots pointing left indicate a club arrived at impact from the outside.

✔ Divots pointing right indicate a club arrived from the inside.

TOM'S SHOTMAKING TIPS

WORKING BACKWARD

The checklist provides a basic list of divots and their cause. When my shot doesn't go as planned, I check my divot, discover the reason, and then work my way back from impact to get myself back on track.

SLIGHT EARLY FACE ROTATION, STEEP DOWNSWING

This divot looks almost perfect but there are two telltale clues. Notice how the divot is nice and long on the toe but comes in a little at the heel as the club exited (1). The face came in square (2) but a slight face rotation (3) started early. The steep downswing clue is the raised grass by the heel (1 and 2). This ball probably hooked left of the target.

D

POINTING LEFT

This is an outside-to-inside divot and the ball sliced. You can see how the outside of the divot has gone so far left (1). This indicates an over-the-top swing that stuck the toe in the ground (2). That's why that portion is so much deeper. Whenever you see this type of divot, work on your transition. Let your hips lead the way, not your shoulders, so you don't come over the top and end up with the toe sticking in the ground when it should be accelerating (3).

POINTING RIGHT

If this is your divot you came into the impact zone too much from the inside and you swung to the outside (1). The ball probably was pushed to the right, although a slight hook is within the realm of possibility. The heel is more dug in (2) and the swing was also a little steep as the divot shows (3).

DRIVER TEE HEIGHT

The ball height is an important element every time I tee it up. Varying the height, depending on the shot needed, allows me to capitalize on the wind direction. Here are three examples and a short checklist to explain my preferences.

TOM'S NORMAL TEE HEIGHT

TEED SLIGHTLY LOWER

For lower drives, like those going into the wind, tee the ball slightly lower.

TEED SLIGHTLY HIGHER

For higher trajectory drives, like those flying with the wind, tee the ball slightly higher.

D

END GAME

Put the ball in the hole! This positive, straight-to-the point, cohesive thought is needed by every golfer regardless of their ability. Putting is covered in the P section, but here we'll offer a couple of drills to instill the "end game" mentality firmly in your mind. One drill is for accuracy and the other for speed.

GOAL POST DRILL

Putting your ball between two goal posts provides an outstanding mental image that can be reinforced during a practice session or before a round.

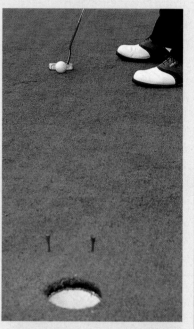

Instead of concentrating on the small hole in the ground, the idea is to putt your ball between the posts.

Starting with a flat putt, your goal posts are two tees placed in the ground less than a hole width apart in front of the hole. Concentrate only on putting the ball between the tees, not on the hole itself.

Putt the ball repeatedly through the goals, and take that thought to the course. For breaking putts, feel the speed you need and then place the tees on the side of the hole the target line arc enters. Score the goal! Put the ball in the hole!

HOLE THE PUTT SPEED DRILL

Chances are your ball often comes up short, robbing you of the chance to make the putt. Even if your line is perfect, the ball can't go in unless you get it there.

How do you ratchet up the speed to correct the problem? Feeling the speed you need to putt the ball over an outstretched club will help you learn to roll the ball firmly enough to give it a chance.

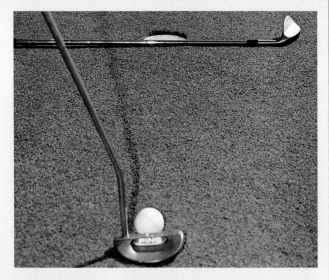

Place a club across your target line, laying it along the edge of the hole. As you address the ball, don't think about the shaft. But change your thoughts as to how firmly you must hit the ball to have it go in after touching the back of the hole.

When you putt the ball with the correct speed it will arrive at the shaft rolling straight and true.

If you hit the putt firmly enough the ball will reach the shaft and hop over it. If you didn't give the ball a chance the shaft will stop it.

Put the ball in the hole! Your ball will hop into the hole over the shaft because you judged, and then executed, the speed correctly. What a positive mental image!

MARTIN'S PRACTICE TEE

While this drill helps you develop a sense of speed it also has some other benefits, especially for short putts.

- On short putts, spike marks and other small undulations will knock your ball off line if the putt is not hit firmly enough.

- The best speed to sink your shorter putts has the ball falling in the hole after first touching the back of the cup.

E

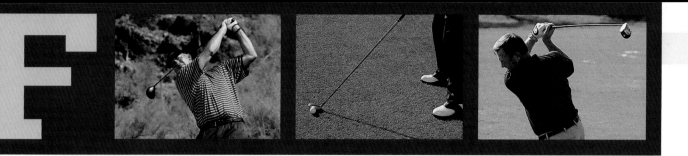

FAIRWAY WOODS

Fairway woods, or more accurately fairway metals, come in various lofts and can replace the harder-to-hit long irons. Used primarily for second shots, these lofted woods are the ideal tools for getting your ball in the best position for an up and down attempt or even to reach the green. The key is to get the ball in the air. Let's investigate with Martin Hall.

PGA TOUR professional Brian Gay launches his 13-degree 3-wood.

Instructor Martin Hall guides you through the intricacies of playing fairway woods.

The primary difficulty in hitting a fairway wood is getting it airborne so the ball can carry the necessary distance. Players struggle with this shot because they either try to hit the ball too hard or hit "up" on it. The results: scooping, or hitting fat shots or drop kicks.

The keys to mastering this important shot include proper ball position and adjusting it for terrain changes, swinging smoothly through the ball to a high follow-through, and getting the feeling of staying behind your swing as long as possible. You may want to jot them down in your golf journal *(section J)* as a reminder before playing the shots. Let's begin with the basic ball position.

BALL POSITION TIP

Ball Position for Driving

As a starting point, position the ball about a ball length back from your driving position (arrow). Ball position is extremely important when hitting a fairway wood.

BALL OPPOSITE LEFT ARMPIT

A good checkpoint is to position the ball opposite your left armpit. This is the lowest point in your swing for this longer club.

UPHILL LIES

Even slight uphill lies require address compensation, because the ball wants to go high naturally. To compensate, move the ball back in your stance slightly.

You also want your hips to aid the swing's sweeping motion, so another adjustment is needed. Pull your left foot slightly back from the line to compensate for the hill.

1 BALL SLIGHTLY BACK

Brian plays the ball slightly back in his stance for even slightly uphill lies. This compensates for the ball wanting to fly on a higher trajectory.

2 PULL LEFT FOOT BACK

Brian drops his left foot back to level his hips. Level hips encourage a sweeping swing.

DOWNHILL LIES

Failing to make these adjustments in your setup from normal lies can unknowingly cause mis-hits. With a downhill lie, the long fairway wood will bottom out sooner—hitting the ground before the ball—unless you make two setup adjustments:

• Play the ball farther back in your stance.

• Bring your right foot back slightly to level your hips.

1 BALL BACK IN STANCE

Brian plays the ball farther back in his stance, understanding that this is the low point of his swing for a downhill lie. The ground comes up sooner.

2 RIGHT FOOT BACK

Fairway wood swings sweep through the ball, and level hips are a factor. To level the hips for this downhill lie, Brian drops his right foot back slightly.

STAYING BEHIND THE BALL

Setting up and swinging smoothly are keys to consistently hitting an uphill or downhill lie with a fairway wood. Feel that the center of your body is staying behind the ball a little longer.

CENTER BEHIND BALL

Making a good shoulder turn, so the back faces the target, keeps the center of Martin's body behind the ball. The length of the backswing also provides enough swing time for the timing elements to come into play. Jerky swings are often the results of very short backswings.

Develop the feeling of staying behind the ball during your backswing and downswing, and all the way to impact.

HIGH FOLLOW-THROUGH

Good fairway woods feature smoothly accelerating swings that stop naturally at the follow-through position. Swinging smoothly, staying behind the ball, rotating around a steady spine and finishing facing your target combine to turn you into a consistently good fairway woods player.

F

FIVE BASIC FUNDAMENTALS

When you incorporate these five basic fundamentals into your game, improvement will be rapid. Writing them in your journal and looking them over before practice or play will program your brain for high level golf. Notice how many parts of the swing the fundamentals apply to.

THE FIVE BASIC FUNDAMENTALS FOR GOOD GOLF

FUNDAMENTAL	DESCRIPTION	REFERRAL FOR DETAILED INFORMATION
1. Grip	Correctly holding the club.	**Grip** in the **G** section.
2. Address	Posture/Alignment/Ball Position.	**Address** in the **A** section. **Posture** in the **P** section. **Alignment** in the **A** section. **Ball Position** in the **B** section.
3. Take-away	Path the club and arms take during the start of the swing.	**Triangle** in the **T** section. **Connected Swing** in the **C** section. **Take-Away** in the **T** section.
4. Steady Head	Head position during the swing maintains the original relationship to the ball formed at address.	**Head** in the **H** section. **Backswing** in the **B** section. **Impact** in the **I** section. **Downswing** in the **D** section. **Follow-Through** in **this** section.
5. Acceleration	Sequence of motion as the clubhead smoothly increases speed throughout the swing.	**Downswing** in the **D** section. **Impact** in the **I** section. **Follow-Through** in **this** section. **Timing and Tempo** in the **T** section.

FLOATER

This shot has very little spin and at one time was a favorite of golfing legend Sam Snead. On long greens he used the floater to get the ball back to the hole, but mostly hit it to confuse opponents about which club he selected.

On a floater, the ball floats through the air, due to the lack of spin, and then stops quickly after landing.

FLUFFY SAND SHOTS

Sand consistency varies and you must adjust your technique accordingly to match the texture. For instance, hard sand needs a soft swing; soft, fluffy sand needs a hard swing.

When the sand is soft and fluffy you need a club with a lot of bounce. Make a bigger swing, propelling the club through the sand with a harder swing.

Hard sand calls for a soft swing. Soft sand calls for a hard swing.

F

FOLLOW-THROUGH

Completing your follow-through while facing the target provides a good indication that you accelerated through the ball and rotated properly. If the ball got in the way of a square clubface at impact, then all is well.

There are some very crucial positions along the follow-through path that make or break your swing, even though the ball has departed. Your follow-through reflects what occurred earlier in the swing, prior to impact. It's the old cause and effect theory. Here, Tom Lehman demonstrates his follow-through and offers some shotmaking tips.

Tom follows through on the 14th hole of The Country Club Course at the DC Ranch in Scottsdale, Arizona.

✔CHECKLIST
FOLLOW-THROUGH

✔ Head remains in place past impact.

✔ Shoulder rotation pulls the head up.

✔ Club reaches full extension past impact.

✔ Wrists release naturally.

✔ You finish facing the target.

TOM'S SHOTMAKING TIPS

SHOT-SHAPING RELEASE

I can control the shape of my shot by the forearm rotation seen in the action photos to follow. Add some hook spin by rotating your right arm over the left. If you want to fade the ball, then hold on a little longer, delaying this rotation and applying a fade spin.

EXTENDED FOLLOW-THROUGH

I'm not controlling the positions you see in the action shot at right; I'm letting them happen naturally. Perfect timing allowed my hips to clear just before impact, letting the club swing through uninterrupted on its swing arc. Clubhead speed increased, and as the club passes through the positions to come, I can coast all the way to the finish.

Notice how steady my head remained. This fixed position was responsible for impacting the ball at the bottom of my pre-set swing arc. The weight has almost totally transferred over to my left side.

Centrifugal force's power extends Tom's club past impact.

FOLLOW-THROUGH EXTENSION

Compare the two follow-through extension positions. Actually only one of the photos qualifies as an extension because the BAD photo shows a premature release before the extension position should occur.

When teachers suggest your grip pressure should be light enough to feel the clubhead as it swings, here's why: The light grip allows the clubhead's weight to cock your wrists naturally on the backswing and uncock them naturally on the follow-through.

GOOD　　*BAD*

Good extension.　　　　*Premature release.*

PARALLEL ARMS, PARALLEL SHAFTS

The shafts should share a common trait during the downswing/follow-through portion of your swing. Notice how the shaft is extended back on the downswing and then forward on the follow-through when the arms reach the parallel-to-the-ground position. This is another indication of power.

DOWNSWING EXTENSION

Shaft extends back.

FOLLOW-THROUGH EXTENSION

Shaft extends forward.

FINISHING THE FOLLOW-THROUGH

The four photos below show how my momentum continues until it runs out of room at the finish position.

Notice how the head is pulled up from its steady position (1) by the shoulder rotation (2 and 3). Finish your follow-through facing the target (4). Any position other than this indicates your hips blocked the arms from swinging the club through on plane.

F

73

GOLF GRASSES

PGA TOUR players encounter various types of grass during the tournament season. In the North, it's the softer bladed bentgrass. In the South, wiry Bermuda grass dominates. Players have their own preference, but to be competitive each week on TOUR they must adjust to both. And new strains are always being introduced.

Weather is the dominant factor in the grass selection process. Bentgrass cannot tolerate high temperatures, but the northern states' cooler climate suits it perfectly. Bermuda loves the heat but not the cold, so on southern courses you'll find it in the summer. During the colder winter months, southern courses must overseed, using varieties of rye grass.

When you watch the western tournaments early in the year the green fairways are dramatically surrounded by yellow grass. Colder winter temperatures cause that grass to go dormant while the overseeded fairways flourish.

SENIOR PGA TOUR professional John Jacobs drives from the tee at the TPC of Scottsdale. During early-season western tournaments, the lush overseeded tees and fairways are surrounded by striking yellow grass that went dormant due to the colder temperatures.

PUTTING AND GRASS

Tom reads the 10th green at the DC Ranch Country Club.

Putting on the various grasses requires adjustments. Softer, finer bentgrass allows a putt to roll truer because the blades grow so close together. Rolling a ball true on Bermuda is a different proposition; each blade is more like a spike and, unlike the carpet-like bentgrass, balls on Bermuda can bump around more due to the sparser growth.

Tiff Eagle, a new strain of grass, is just as heat tolerant as Bermuda but grows closer together like bent and is getting rave reviews from those who have putted on it. Tiff Eagle is also equally fast for the morning and afternoon tournament rounds.

READING THE GRAIN

When you putt it's important to check the direction the grass is growing. With bentgrass this is not always as important as it is with Bermuda.

✔CHECKLIST
READING THE GRAIN

✔ Bermuda grass greens grow in the direction of the setting sun.

✔ Putts toward the setting sun will be faster, while those away from that direction will be slower.

✔ A steep slope on a Bermuda green will make the grass grow in the direction of the water flow off the green.

✔ Checking both sides of the cup will tell you the direction of the grass grain at the hole.

✔ The smooth side is *with* the grain while the rough edge is *against* the grain.

G

GRIPS

It's obvious that grips connect your body to the club, but *how* they connect the body to the club makes or breaks your golf swing. Hands set incorrectly will not allow the clubface to be square at impact.

Just as their swings vary, PGA TOUR professionals also use a variety of grips. Jack Nicklaus has used an interlocking grip over the years with phenomenal success, while Tom and a host of professionals prefer the overlapping variety of grip. You need to find one that works best for you. Tom shows you some options here, along with a few shotmaking tips.

Tom's grip is like his printer cable to the club—fully functional and transmitting perfect information. An incorrect grip is like a defective cable: the swing would end up looking like gibberish.

A WORD ABOUT GRIPS

Tom shows Jack Nicklaus's grip preference—the interlocking grip.

All of your feel comes from holding onto the club with your hands. So what's the ideal grip for you? If you were just starting out then I would suggest a classic grip like the interlocking or the overlapping.

Ben Hogan's grip was a classic example because it was neutral. All good grips share the opposing hand similarity; the hands are opposite each other as the club is gripped. Palms should be facing each other so the hands can work together instead of fighting each other.

Having equal pressure on both sides of the club is highly desirable. A bad example is having pressure on the left side and a right hand slightly underneath that is exerting unbalanced pressure. This grip is out of whack.

On TOUR you see some players with very strong grips (the V's formed between the thumb and forefinger of each hand are pointing to the right shoulder) and some players with very weak grips (the V's point to the left shoulder). But because both hands are that way they are balanced and applying equal pressure to both sides of the clubhead.

TOM'S GRIP

I have a fairly weak left hand and a stronger right hand, yet my grip is pretty well balanced. It's not a classically perfect grip by any means, but the key is it works for me!

If your grip works for you then who cares what it looks like. There have been a whole group of successful players in this game who have very funky grips. You learn to swing in a manner that accommodates the grip.

Here's what you won't see—a player with a real strong grip

Although not a classic grip, because the left hand is weaker than the right, Tom's grip works for him. He suggests you stick with a grip that works for you.

who has a strong release of his hands. A duck hook would be the result.

Paul Azinger has a strong grip but he hangs onto it, delaying the rotation. He can hit fades from a grip that would normally produce controllable draws.

But if you're a beginner, or teaching a child or friend who is a beginner, start off with a classical grip. On the other hand, if you've played golf forever and your grip is a certain way with a swing that produces a consistent ball flight and shape, then I wouldn't advise changing anything.

If you are a poor player and part of the problem is a poor grip, causing you to make plenty of moves in your swing to accommodate it, then you need to start over. It's time for the old rebuild job, returning to the basics.

HOW TO GRIP THE CLUB

Gripping your club correctly permits the free-flowing swing needed to produce distance and accuracy. Positioning the left and right hands properly creates a balanced harmony that allows your wrists to hinge and unhinge naturally. As the clubface is swung down to the ball, a correct grip makes it possible for the club to arrive square to the target line.

LEFT HAND

Lay the club diagonally across the base of the left fingers and across the palm. Be sure to allow the butt of the club to extend past your left hand about a half inch.

RIGHT HAND

The right hand holds the club mostly in your fingers. This significantly increases your sense of feel. Grip the club with the right hand at the base of the fingers where they meet the palm. Do not grab the club tightly; ease into the position, encouraging a tension-free grip.

CLOSED GRIP

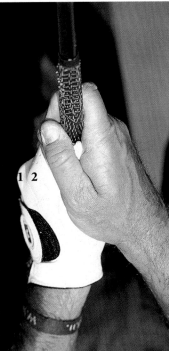

When you close the grip you must be able to see two knuckles on your left hand. (1, 2) If you see three knuckles the grip is too strong (too much to the right side of the club), and you will hook the ball. Should you see only one knuckle the grip is too weak (too much to the left side of the club), and you will slice the ball.

Check to see that the V's are pointing to inside of your right shoulder (left shoulder for left-handed golfers.).

G

GRIP: LONG AND SHORT THUMBS

Adjust the length of your left thumb to customize your shotmaking ability in your long game.

LONG THUMB = MORE ACCURACY

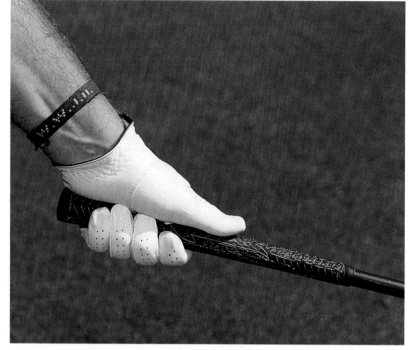

With your left thumb in an extended position on the grip, you are in the accuracy grip position. The longer thumb tightens up the left wrist and forearm, which should produce a slight fade and a more accurate drive.

SHORT THUMB = MORE DISTANCE

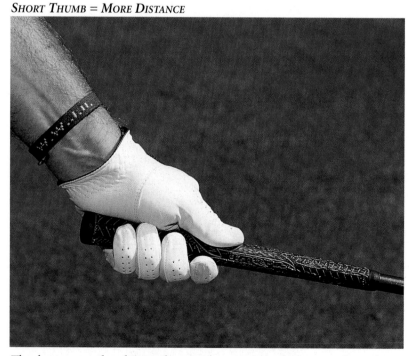

The shorter your thumb is on the grip, the more wrist flex you can have. A short left thumb promotes wrist action, which in turn creates clubhead speed. Shorter thumbs also promote more of a hook swing, which is beneficial if you tend to slice.

OVERLAP OR INTERLOCK

I prefer an overlapping grip, but John Daly, like Jack Nicklaus, interlocks the little finger of his right hand with his left forefinger. Try both and see which one works for you.

TOM'S OVERLAPPING GRIP

JOHN DALY'S INTERLOCKING GRIP

GRIP PRESSURE

If I feel my forearms tensing, I know I'm gripping the club too tightly. On the other hand, if the club is going all over the place in my swing, then I know my grip pressure is too loose. The key is to feel enough pressure to get good control of the club ... but don't feel tension building into anxiety.

Tension destroys a free-flowing, centrifugal-force swing. Arm tension prevents the free flow from propelling the clubhead around the wide swing arc. Balanced pressure works best.

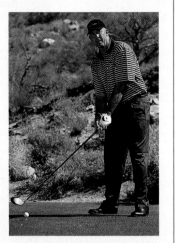

Tom adjusts his grip pressure while checking his target.

TOM'S SHOTMAKING TIPS

CURING PROBLEMS

All of us lapse into swing problems from time to time. Learn to recognize the symptoms and treat them before they become ingrained in your game. All through this book we refer to "feel" and being aware when things don't feel quite right.

The brain finds comfort levels. If the initial alert is ignored and the problem not cured, a new feeling takes over and that's the one you don't want. If the brain gets comfortable with something, it makes it that much harder to cure the problem.

BALANCED PRESSURE

A tension-free grip controls the club by balancing the pressure on both sides of the club.

LEFT HAND GRIP PRESSURE

The last three fingers of your left hand feel the pressure for control. Right hand grip pressure should be just enough to balance the left.

DRILL

TOM'S TWO-FINGER OFF DRILL

Whenever I feel my grip pressure getting too strong, it's time for the Two-Finger Off Drill. You can try this on the range or for some of your practice swings. It reinforces the correct grip pressure needed for a free-flowing swing.

Taking the right thumb and index finger off the shaft programs the feel for a tension-free grip. Hit some balls on the range using this drill and then some with the fingers on the club.

G

HARDPAN SHOT

Hardpan can mean different things depending on where you're playing golf. Florida's hardpan, with its sandy subsoil, differs from courses in the Northeast where clay soils produce hard, tight lies.

For the sake of this topic, let's refer to these shots as tight lies since all share a common similarity: the difficulty of hitting off a bare, hard surface.

TIGHT LIE

Hard surfaces are like backboards. Your club can bounce off them, causing a skulled shot. The best shotmaking tip with this shot— and all shots—is to maintain a very still body throughout the swing, limiting the chance for a mis-hit.

THE GOAL

Tight lie shots have less backspin, fly lower and run longer as a result. Landing in longer grass applies a braking action.

CHOOSE A LANDING AREA

SENIOR PGA TOUR star Bruce Fleisher plays the shot by selecting a landing area in the fringe around the green. His goal is to reach this spot, which will scrub off some speed before the ball rolls to the pin.

✔CHECKLIST
TIGHT LIE SHOTS

✔ Select a landing point.

✔ Select a club.

✔ Position ball in the middle of your stance with hands positioned forward.

✔ Keep your head and body still throughout the swing.

✔ Use an arm-dominated swing.

SETUP

Bruce's hands are ahead of the clubhead.

You must *pick this shot*. A clean hit begins by properly setting up. Using a lofted club, Bruce positions the ball in the middle of his stance with his hands forward.

Creating some loft is possible, but be careful. The bounce of a wedge doesn't contribute to thinning or skulling the shot.

TOM'S SHOTMAKING ALERT

SHAFT POSITION

When you set up to hit a hardpan or tight lie shot, be sure that your shaft angles forward like Bruce's. If the shaft is perpendicular to the ground or, even worse, angled away from the ball, the lower portion of the club will bounce into the ball and skull it.

Improper shaft alignment comes from a desire to help the ball into the air by lifting it. This shot requires a descending blow for a clean impact. Remember: Hands forward = shaft forward.

QUIET BODY

Hardpan and other tight lie shots require precision at impact. You need to *pick the shot*, impacting it cleanly without the clubhead bouncing into the ball.

The arm-dominated swing limits lower body motion. Combined with a very still head and quiet body, the fundamentals for hitting a *pick* are in place. Stay in control as you swing.

Limiting your backswing (1) to stay in control is one way to maintain a quiet body for this shot. Any unnecessary movement will detract from the clean impact (2) you need.

THE RESULTS

Bruce played this Florida hardpan shot perfectly. He picked it, landed it on his target and it's rolling to the pin.

H

HEAD

Fat shots, topped shots and misses to the left and right are symptoms of a head that moves during the swing. Head movement relocates the swing's low spot, and a variety of bad outcomes are possible as a result. All great ball strikers feel their head remains steady throughout the swing. While there must be some movement, they feel the head is steady.

This is so important that many teachers list a steady head as one of golf's five basic fundamentals. It's because the head is the center of the swing; everything revolves around it.

Moving the head requires compensations by your brain to get the club back to the ball. That's not a recipe for accuracy and power.

John Daly takes the club back way beyond parallel when he drives. Even with more than average motion he still maintains a steady head. Imagine how difficult it would be to get back to the ball if he moved his head up and down or left and right.

HIGH FADES

Fades, by their very nature, tend to fly higher than hooks. The open-at-impact clubface increases clubhead loft. A left-to-right combination of back and sidespin also contributes to elevating and curving the shot. Tom takes us through it.

✔ CHECKLIST
HITTING HIGH FADES

✔ Aim the club at your target.

✔ Open your stance.

✔ Swing along your foot line.

✔ Delay forearm rotation past impact.

✔ Finish high.

OPEN SETUP

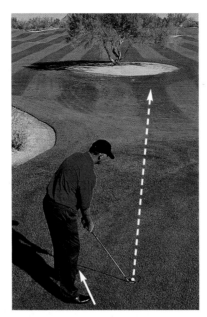

This is a classic, open setup to the target. The clubface is aligned square to the target line (just right of the tree), but Tom's foot line points to the left (arrow). Swinging along the foot line creates a high fade because of impacting the ball from the right to the left.

IMPACT

The divot direction clearly indicates the swing plane is following the foot line (arrow). Impact occurred with an open clubface and the shot will curve as it flies from left to right.

SWING PLANE

The toe of Tom's club is pointing way to the left of the tree as he reaches the top of his backswing. Return to the ball along this plane, aligned to your foot line, to create an open clubface at impact.

FINISH HIGH

A high finish and delayed arm rotation ensured that the ball left the ground with a left-to-right rotational backspin. Had Tom incorrectly rotated the arms early while swinging along the foot line, the ball would be travelling straight to the left instead of curving to the right, up and around the tree.

You can also use this same shotmaking technique to hit high fades off the tee or fairway with woods and long irons.

H

IMPACT

Moment of truth! The entire essence of your swing is judged in the mere 1/1000 of a second when the club and ball meet. Yet impact is not a controllable position. It is merely a reaction to what occurred before it and, to a certain extent, after it.

Amateur golfers are so intent on this one moment—actually hitting the ball—that the significance of its true meaning is never learned. But PGA TOUR players such as Tom Lehman understand impact. They realize it's only a brief moment in their golf swing when the ball got in the way. The quality impact you strive for is based on five basic fundamentals for a good golf swing. They are the only checklist you need for impact.

SENIOR PGA TOUR player John Jacobs at impact.

✔CHECKLIST
IMPACT

✔ **Grip.** Hold the club correctly.

✔ **Address.** Consider posture, alignment and ball position.

✔ **Take-away.** Plan the path the club and arms take during the start of the swing.

✔ **Steady Head.** Maintain the original relationship to the ball that was formed at address.

✔ **Acceleration.** Follow the sequence of motion as the clubhead smoothly increases speed throughout the swing.

IMPACT ELEMENTS

My positions through the impact zone point out some very important elements found in better golfers' swings. I'll go into each in depth but as a starting point read this list and refer to the combined action shot below.

1 Delay impact.

2 Shift weight properly.

3 Keep a steady head.

4 Maintain your power triangle.

5 Maintain wrist angles through impact.

Tom Lehman drives through the impact zone.

DELAYED IMPACT

If it looks like my clubhead is lagging behind (right), you're right. The lower body starts the transition to the downswing and the clubhead, having farther to travel, will only catch up at impact as it accelerates rapidly through the ball, almost like whipping it through. The grip is in front of my chest and the triangle formed by my shoulder line, arms and hands powerfully pulls the clubhead along the swing plane.

If the clubhead were *ahead* at this stage, it means the club was thrown from the top and the wrists released too early. Instead, this delayed hit produces extra speed and more distance.

RETURNING THE POWER TRIANGLE TO ADDRESS

As the club enters the impact zone (right), you can see how the power triangle remains intact, as it does throughout my swing. With the grip in front of my chest, all the timing elements rhythmically come together in time for the approaching crucial moment. Here are some other important points:

- The hips are slightly turned to the left, showing that I am accelerating through the ball and not at it.

- The hands are leading the clubhead into the impact zone. If the hands pass the clubhead you have slowed down, causing a loss of power and path.

- Notice how my steady head has stayed back, allowing the clubhead's natural centrifugal force to swing powerfully through.

- My raised right heel indicates the weight is almost totally transferred to my left side. Weight is power's fuel and it was stored on the right side on the backswing, ready to transfer back to acceleration and great impact.

PAST IMPACT

The clubhead swings through the ball to this point in the impact zone. Notice that as I sweep through the ball my head stays back allowing the clubhead to powerfully accelerate through this critical zone.

WHEN DRIVING A NAIL, DO YOU STAND IN FRONT OR BACK OF IT?

The power position is *behind* the ball, as Martin Hall's teaching aid illustrates. It's a golf ball sticking out the back of a piece of wood with a tee.

Martin's aid illustrates that, just like hammering a nail, the proper impact position requires staying behind while applying the force. Are you guilty of losing power by moving forward as you swing, instead of maintaining a power body position? The drill below should help.

DRILL

UNWIND DRILL

Placing a ball on top of an old shaft and linking your body turn to knock it off develops the feeling for staying behind the ball at impact. Hold your driver across your chest, as I do below.

Rotate and wind up away from the ball. Feel the coiling of power as you turn away.

Unwind your body and knock the teed-up ball off the shaft. The key is keeping your face behind the shaft through impact.

I

INTERMEDIATE TARGET

The place you want the ball to end up isn't the only target you need to consider. Sometimes a point part way there is equally as important to your shot's success.

INTERMEDIATE TARGET: LONG GAME

Trying to line your body up to a distant target can cost accuracy. Pick out a spot along the target line and align your clubhead to it. Next, align your body along a parallel line. As you swing you will have the confidence that you are accurately lined up for the shot.

Tom's intermediate target is circled. Having a closer spot to aim to makes alignment easier and more accurate.

INTERMEDIATE TARGET: PUTTING

Selecting an intermediate target for putting can be a stumbling block for less-skilled players. Choosing a closer target along a straight line to the hole dooms the effort because very few putts are totally straight. The key is aligning to a target on the line the ball starts on, and not the hole.

JIM FURYK'S INTERMEDIATE TARGET

Jim Furyk knows better than to align himself to the hole for breaking putts. He chose an intermediate target (X) on the path the ball starts on, and aligns to that point. Now he only has to concentrate on speed.

DAVE STOCKTON'S INTERIM TARGET

In the photo, Dave's putter is on his interim target. Once he returns the club back behind the ball he only focuses on this interim target, not the ball. The next time he sees the ball it's rolling over the interim target.

Dave's Interim Target

SENIOR PGA TOUR veteran Dave Stockton, one of the best putters of all time, has a unique interim target. His clubhead is touching it here. It's located only an inch in front of his ball.

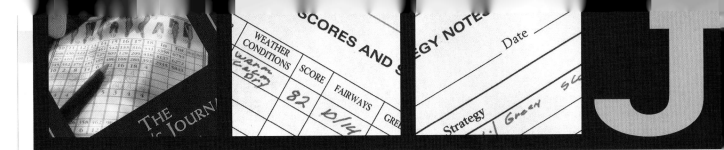

JOURNAL

If you are truly dedicated to improving your game, the very first item you need to buy is not the hot new teaching aid you just saw on some TV infomercial. What you really need is a golf journal—a small book that fits in your bag and helps you keep tabs on your statistics and practice sessions, and also provides room for notes.

When you find something that works, be it a change in ball position, a reminder to keep your shoulders parallel to the target line at address or just a swing thought, the journal is right there to keep you up to speed on your game.

THE
GOLFER'S JOURNAL

SAMPLE STATISTIC PAGES

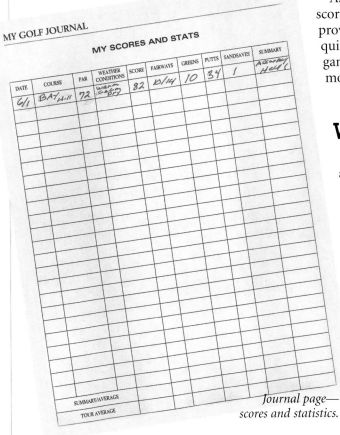

DATE	COURSE	PAR	WEATHER CONDITIONS	SCORE	FAIRWAYS	GREENS	PUTTS	SANDSAVES	SUMMARY
6/1	BAY H.H	72	warm calm dry	82	10/14	10	34	1	A General Help

MY GOLF JOURNAL
MY SCORES AND STATS

SUMMARY/AVERAGE
TOUR AVERAGE

Journal page—scores and statistics.

As you play your round make notes on the scorecard. Transferring them to your golf journal provides a continuous record of your statistics. You'll quickly identify trends pointing at the parts of your game needing the most help. Let's look at some of the more important categories of information.

WEATHER

This is an important entry because weather can adversely affect even the best golfers' games. Your score on a windy day will most likely be several shots higher because accuracy and length suffer. That's not to say you can't profit by playing in the wind. Staying in control and not forcing shots will help you later in good weather conditions.

On warm days the ball travels farther, and in dry weather the greens are usually harder and faster. Professionals factor in all this information for club selection, targeting purposes (both in the fairway and on approach shots to the green) and for judging the speed of their putts. Low scores are not derived from chance or luck; they require skill and paying attention to even the smallest details.

J

FAIRWAYS

You want to keep track of fairways hit and driving accuracy. Did your ball remain in the fairway off the tee? Using this kind of information can let you quickly hone in on your long game accuracy.

For example, on a par-72 course with four par-3 holes subtracted, there are 14 opportunities to land in the fairway. This golfer (page 87) hit 10 of them for a percentage of 71.4.

On the PGA TOUR, 68.5 percent is the average of fairways hit during a round. The category leader hit 79.7 percent one recent year. A ball could be just lying in the first cut of rough and in great shape but it still missed the fairway. Pros work the ball more, seldom hitting a straight shot, so the spin may just take the ball off the fairway after landing, or maybe they hit it too well or curved it too much.

GREENS

This heading refers to Greens In Regulation (GIR). The statistics work on the assumption that you reached the green in the number of strokes that would allow a birdie putt. For example:

PAR	GIR
Par 3	1
Par 4	2
Par 5	3

The golfer on page 87 reached 10 greens in regulation (56.5 %) compared to the PGA TOUR average 66% (category leader 75.2%). Some additional work on approach shots would seem to be needed. Misses required a pitch or chip to get back into position on the green. Instead of putting for birdie, he was putting for par. If that putt was missed, another stoke over par was added to the score.

PUTTS

Our golfer took 34 putts to hole out, an average of 1.9 strokes per hole. The average on the PGA TOUR is 1.77. Stats like this need to be evaluated with chipping or pitching performance information to determine the length faced for most of his putts. Did you hole some first putts and three-putt others? Add these types of notes to provide a clear record.

A journal provides important statistics on how efficiently you reached the green, and then holed out.

A JOURNAL IS ESSENTIAL!

In the notes, page 87's golfer added "accuracy help!" Accuracy is an area even professionals work on continuously, and points out the problem that he felt most affected his score.

But is it a trend or just a new problem that showed up that day? The record of his other rounds would show that immediately. So you see, a golf journal allows you to pick up on problems before they become embedded in your game.

COURSE STRATEGY NOTES

Another important golf journal benefit is jotting down your strategy for playing specific holes on specific courses. PGA TOUR professionals don't re-invent the wheel every year. They keep notes on yardage and strategy to use as starting points for when they play the course next.

Golf is an intelligent game for intelligent people, and every bit of information collected boosts your confidence to fully commit to a shot. Never hit a shot that you are not totally committed to or your next shot will be a *trouble shot*.

COURSE STRATEGY NOTES

Golf Course _____

Date _____

Hole #	Strategy
1	Right Side Bunker—Draw Away.
2	5 - iron (2nd Shot) Green Slopes R To G
3	
4	
5	
6	
7	
8	
9	
10	
11	
12	
13	
14	
15	
16	
17	
18	

Comments:

91

A golf journal provides insights into course strategies that worked before.

PRACTICE SESSIONS

Time is a precious commodity for all golfers. To maximize the time you have for practice, have a clear understanding of what you want to work on and accomplish. For example, if you're working on mastering a basic fundamental, your practice session needs to be organized. A golf journal lets you do that.

Taking the notes from your rounds into consideration, a practice session comprised of timed segments can be constructed, placing emphasis on where work is needed the most. Once a problem is corrected, your notes on *how* that was accomplished provide a fast cure should the problem reappear.

Make sure your journal fits in your bag so it's on hand when needed the most.

J

KNOCKDOWN SHOT

"Knock-the-trajectory-down shot" would be the full definition of this shot, which good golfers rely on for a variety of situations. Maybe you have to go under a tree branch but still need enough power to roll the ball on the green after it lands short. Hitting a lower-trajectory shot when the wind is blowing with or against you can be a control and accuracy advantage too.

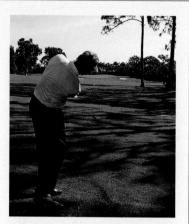

When you are between 100 and 150 yards of the pin, being able to effectively play the knockdown shot can get you on the green even if the wind is blowing or obstacles are in your way.

Understanding how to control a ball's trajectory to fit your needs, and then developing the technique to pull off the shot successfully, is what playing exceptional golf is all about. Maintaining control of your game while eliminating the variables makes for solid golf, as Martin Hall demonstrates.

Martin Hall's knockdown shot at impact.

The normal technique for long or middle iron play needs to be modified to knock the trajectory of the ball down yet still provide controlled power, accuracy and distance.

When everything comes together perfectly the ball will fly on a lower, flatter trajectory than it normally would have with my regular swing. Backspin is at a minimum. Try these adaptations to master this shot.

STAND CLOSER

Stand slightly closer to the ball. The club on the ground represents where your heels would be for a normal iron shot.

GRIP PRESSURE

Increase the grip pressure of the last three fingers on your left hand. This firmer-than-normal pressure keeps loft off the shot by dragging the club through impact.

BALL BACK IN STANCE

Play the ball back in your stance. This limits the loft the club can have at impact; the trajectory will be lower.

UNWINDING THE HIPS

Using your hips correctly is key to making a good knockdown shot.

1 Because the body does not move as much as it does during a full swing, you may have a tendency to hook the shot at first. To correct this problem keep your hips unwinding through the shot.

2 If the hips don't move through impact, the arms will cross over resulting in a hook. Practicing this shot on the range builds your confidence before using it during a round.

THE KNOCKDOWN SWING

1- ADDRESS

The ball is a little farther back in your stance than it would be for a regular full swing shot. All through this sequence you will observe how the head remains virtually in the same position, using the white "T-pole" in the background as a reference point.

As the center of the golf swing, your head and spine must remain in position as you rotate. Should they move up or down or off the ball, it's impossible to get back at impact in the same position you were at address.

2- BACKSWING EXTENSION

Even for this knockdown shot, the swing arc must still be as wide as possible. Check Martin's head position. It's virtually in the same position relative to the T-pole. There is only the slightest bit of movement and the head remains steady.

3- BACKSWING

The swing triangle, made up of the hands, arms and chest, remains intact. Notice how the grip of the club is in front of the chest. The head is in the same position, the wrists are cocking and the toe of the club is pointing in the air.

4- COMBINED POSITIONS

This combined photo shows the top of the partial backswing and how the rotation of the hips toward the target has brought the arms and club down. No need to over-swing into a parallel-to-the-ground position for this partial shot. Notice the head is in the same position as it was at address.

The hips should resist winding up on the backswing but keep unwinding through the downswing. The torque created by the hips builds power while their continuous unwinding movement through the shot prevents the arms from crossing in front of them, which could cause a hook.

K

5- IMPACT

The swing created this position at impact. This 5-iron looks like the clubhead of a 1-iron as it impacts the ball. Wrists are firm and have not released early. The trajectory has to be lower because additional backspin is not being applied to the ball.

Notice that even though weight has transferred over to the target side of the body, the spine remains behind the ball.

6- RETURN TO ADDRESS AT IMPACT

With impact position superimposed you can see how the address position was re-created at that crucial moment. The hips have rotated but arms, chest and grip are in the power triangle. Head and spine are steady and in the same position even though the body rotated completely away from the ball and then powerfully returned.

Can you control body movement back to this position if you swayed or tilted off the shot? No, you can't physically put yourself back in the same position; you have to maintain it as you swing. This comes from setting up with good posture at address. Only then can the positions be comfortably and reliably maintained throughout your swing.

POST IMPACT

HIP HIGH PAST IMPACT

The wrists have not uncocked but are firm past impact. Any premature release would add backspin to the ball. Backspin creates higher trajectories, not lower ones. Notice the power triangle established at address and maintained throughout this connected golf swing.

PARTIAL FOLLOW-THROUGH

This is all the follow-through you need for this partial swing. Over-swinging creates physical elements that make the ball fly higher as a result of the air interacting with the faster-moving ball's dimples. Keep the swing under control.

LANDING AREA

Top-level golfers never purposely leave anything to chance. They meticulously plot their attack on a given hole. Playing to their strengths limits potential errors and mis-hits.

Targeted landing areas are chosen based on the line players feel create birdie opportunities. For the most part, they prefer playing full shots into a green as opposed to partial swing attempts. This limits the margin for error.

Landing areas are crucial because they impact distance remaining, incline (if any), and your line to the hole. Using the DC Ranch's 10th hole, Tom takes you through his process of selecting a targeted landing area.

Play to your strengths by choosing landing areas that complement your ability instead of challenging it. Seen above is the perfect approach shot landing area for the TPC of Sawgrass's 16th hole.

L

TOM'S SELECTION PROCESS

Tom's drive to his targeted landing area (circled) on the 385-yard 10th hole.

When I play any hole, I think about what I do best. Sticking to that concept is how my hole strategy is plotted. Off the tee, the entire fairway is not my landing target; the smaller circled area (left) is.

Looking at this hole before teeing off, I decided to hit my approach shot from the right side of the fairway. I drive the ball 285 yards, so the bunkers are not going to be a problem and the fairway is nice and flat on the right side, making it an easy full sand wedge into the green.

With my targeted landing area programmed in my mind, I aimed at the left side of the big tree (I don't aim to a spot on the ground; distant objects on that line work better), playing a slight draw to reach the landing area best suited for my approach shot.

LANDING AREA

This flat landing area was the designated target, providing the perfect line for the next shot to the green. This line works for some golfers, but remember to always play to your strengths!

TOM'S SHOTMAKING TIPS

KNOW YOUR OWN ABILITIES

When you look at a hole's yardage, determine if you have the length to reach the green in regulation. If you know you need three strokes instead of two to reach a par-4, you need an interim landing target, between your drive and your third shot. That still provides your best line to the hole.

Employ this strategy on par-5 holes too. Working your way back from the hole identifies the areas that provide the best opportunity to get from point to point along your most favorable line.

LAY-UP SHOT

Lay-up shots were anathema to Arnold Palmer during the height of his career. The King endeared himself to the golfing public by shunning any temptation to surrender to a hole, preferring to bend it to his will and conquer it. His career and life provide the perfect definition for the term "risk and reward."

Arnie won 60 times, but as Lee Trevino, his friend and competitor over the years, says, "He probably lost that many with that *go for it* philosophy, but he wouldn't have won that many in the first place by not playing to his strengths."

But lay-up shots for mere mortals do make sense and deserve consideration as part of any shot-saving strategy. Adding an extra stroke by not going for the green may save you additional strokes by keeping you out of a hazard and suffering penalty stokes. Laying up to a comfortable distance provides the confidence for playing an easier shot and finishing close to the pin.

On this long dogleg par-5 hole, playing a lay-up shot is a wise strategical decision.

✔CHECKLIST
LAY-UP SHOTS

✔ Determine the *risk* and the *reward* for the shot under consideration.

✔ If it's all *risk and risk*, a better choice is to lay up, playing less club or a partial shot instead.

✔ Identify your lay-up landing target as a place where you would prefer playing your next shot from.

✔ Mentally commit to the lay-up shot, putting *what might have been* out of your mind.

✔ Swing easily, concentrating on feeling your rhythm.

L

LEG DRIVE

The photos used in this section have been shaded to keep your eyes focused strictly on Tom's lower body. A powerful leg drive leads the way, pulling the upper body along with it, as Tom explains in this section.

LEGS LEAD THE WAY

The series of photos will show you how my legs have taken over the primary responsibility for powering the swing.

Tom's lower body provided solid support for the backswing. But all through the downswing it led the charge back and through the ball.

1- ALMOST TO THE TOP

Notice the bend in Tom's left knee, indicating weight has been transferred almost totally to the other leg. In a split second the left knee and hip will start back toward the ball while the upper body continues on the backswing. The shirt wrinkles show the wound-up energy.

2- LEG DRIVE UNDERWAY

Notice how Tom's lower body has started rotating toward the ball. The left knee is straightening as the weight transfers over, fueling the power available that is being transmitted through the big thigh muscles. Leg drive is providing the energy for centrifugal force.

As the club enters the impact zone from slightly inside the line, leg drive is clearing the hips. Space for the arms to swing the club through on plane is vital to accuracy and distance. Leg drive creates the slightly open-to-the-target-line lower body position at impact.

4- Follow-Through

Leg drive is powering the lower body rotation all the way to the follow-through position. At the finish, hips should be facing the target.

LINE TO THE HOLE

Every golfer should tackle holes with the desire to make the lowest score possible. Obvious, right? Well, unless you have chosen a line with landing targets along the way, you may be the one who's tackled for a loss.

Consult the Z section to learn how you can avoid the Z factor and play the best line for your game by utilizing grid target golf. The score doesn't know if you played the hole on the same line as Tom Lehman. Play the hole with positions and lines suitable for *your* game.

Higher handicappers can partially make up for their game quality by being even smarter planning the strategy. Pick lines and lay-up points to keep you in the hunt. Never just hit balls as hard as you can and allow fate to decide the position of your next shot.

Control or be controlled. Remember that in golf nothing happens until you hit the ball. Time is on your side to plan.

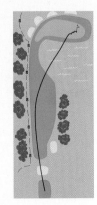

Players should choose the line to the hole providing their best opportunity to score. Strategically, you must know this line to pick out landing targets.

TWO DIFFERENT LINES

PRO LINE

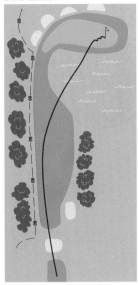

On Bay Hill's 18th hole, this is the line a pro might choose. Knowing your line provides needed input for the side of the tee box to hit your drive from.

REGULAR GUY LINE

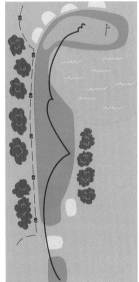

Playing the same hole, this might be the line of a higher handicap player. Avoiding several hazards is important. Choosing the correct line helps you play safe. Remember: Always play to your strengths for lower scores!

L

LOB SHOTS

Whenever you need a short, high and soft landing shot, it's great to have a lob or flop shot in your arsenal. Phil Mickelson may be the dean of the lob, playing the ball forward in his stance and using a club with hardly any bounce. His full swing for a shot that close makes little sense to some people unless they realize the physics involved.

A lofted club propels the ball high in the air but not far. The longer Phil swings, the higher it goes. In fact, the clubhead passes the climbing ball immediately after impact, as Tom demonstrates here.

Tom's lofted clubface is about to slide under the ball, propelling it high in the air for a soft landing.

When you play a lob or flop shot, use whichever club you are the most comfortable with. I'm pretty much a one-wedge player, so if I have a shot that needs to go a little bit higher and softer I just open the face, adding additional loft.

For example, with a 60-yard shot that needs to fly high and land soft, I open the blade of my 56-degree wedge and aim a little left.

A lob shot is like a cut shot in that respect. That's why it's very important to understand the amount of bounce you have in your wedges. The more you open the face the more bounce is added, and with that the potential to skull the shot is increased.

Phil Mickelson grew up practicing for hours hitting the lob shots we all admire so much. But he uses a wedge that has almost no bounce. Phil plays with two or three wedges in the bag, using his short game strength, while my game thrives on carrying an extra wood in the bag or a 1-iron instead.

1- TOP OF THE BACKSWING

A big, "syrupy" swing is the best way to get the ball way up in the air. Before the swing starts, at address, you should:

• *Play the ball up in your stance.*

• *Open the face before gripping.*

• *Aim slightly left of your target.*

• *Slightly open your stance.*

2- LOWER BODY LEADS THE WAY

Accuracy is important, and it's a mistake to allow your upper body to lead the way. Make sure your lower body begins the transition back toward the ball, pulling the upper body along into the swing.

3- SLIDE UNDER THE BALL

Just prior to impact, the open clubface approaches the ball. Don't try to help the ball by lifting your swing. Instead, slip the clubhead under the ball, allowing the built-in loft to work for you.

4- CLUB PASSES THE BALL

The clubhead will pass the ball at this stage. Unlike distance shots where clubhead speed and impact firmly smack the ball toward the target, lob shots slide under the ball instead.

The ball rolls up the lofted clubface as the grooves grab it, creating backspin. As a result, the clubhead momentum takes it past the climbing ball.

5- HIGH FOLLOW-THROUGH

When you hear the term "high follow-through," that does not mean you lift the body up through the shot. Notice how Tom's head has remained in position (1), maintaining spine angle. This allows the clubhead loft to perform its task without trying to help the ball into the air.

The arms- and hands-high finish (2) is a good indication that plenty of backspin was put on the ball. Notice how similar the finish position is to the top of the backswing position (inset).

LOOSE LIES

Not all lies are perfect and occasionally you end up in a loose lie situation. Instead of using the *old foot wedge*, rise to the occasion by mastering the shotmaking techniques needed for playing this shot successfully. Frank Lickliter is going to help us here.

Frank Lickliter plays a shot off loose pine straw.

1- AVOID PENALTIES!

Whenever you play a shot off of a loose lie, be careful not to cause the ball to move. If it rolls after you grounded the club you must add a penalty stroke and replace the ball.

✔CHECKLIST
LOOSE LIES

✔ Open the clubface for shorter shots.

✔ Do not cause the ball to roll. Do not ground your club.

✔ Relax your hands. This is a hands-dominated shot.

✔ Hands lead the backswing.

✔ Relax your grip on the downswing. This allows your hands to slip the clubface under the ball.

2- HANDS LEAD THE WAY

Frank Lickliter's arms are remaining still as he takes the club away with his hands. Notice how the wrist angle departs for the one-piece take-away incorporated in most swings.

3- PARTIAL BACKSWING

You need to stay in control. Allow the feel for the distance to determine the actual length of your backswing, but for most shots only a partial backswing is necessary.

4- SLOW AND SMOOTH

Pros swing slowly, which accounts for their superior hand and eye coordination. Playing this shot requires a slow, smooth swing to allow the clubface to slip under the ball.

LOW FADE
See Shaping Shots in Section S

LOW RUNNING LONG IRON
See Knockdown Shot in Section K

LOW TRAJECTORY DRIVE
See Driver Tee Height in Section D

L

MIDDLE IRONS

Once you're within a middle iron's range, laser like accuracy is your goal. Regardless of the length of the hole from the tees, with a middle iron in hand you are basically playing a par-3 hole's distance. Getting up and down is an achievable goal. Martin Hall has three drills to tune your swing plane for improved middle iron accuracy.

Tom Lehman's middle iron swing sends the ball toward the target with laser-like accuracy.

TOM'S SHOTMAKING TIPS

Three clubs form the middle iron grouping:

5-iron - 150 to 175 yards

6-iron - 140 to 160 yards

7-iron - 130 to 150 yards

MIDDLE IRON TRILOGY

Three clubs are generally considered to be the middle irons, and their scoring potency is totally dependent on your accuracy. The distances listed at left are averages. Your swing plane must be superior to return the clubface back square to the target line at impact, unless purposely working the ball was the objective.

For example, over the top swing planes (an outside-to-in swing path) will either pull the ball way to the left or slice it to the right. In either case a long pitch back to the green, instead of a putt, is the penalty paid for inaccurate middle iron shots.

SWING PLANE SWEETSPOT DRILL

Swing plane accuracy controls shot distance and accuracy. It's all important once you are in middle iron territory. This outstanding drill maintains swing plane perfection. The best part is you can do it in your backyard, keeping your swing sharp.

Ideally, the club and ball should meet on the iron's sweetspot instead of the toe or heel. Substituting three tees for your ball places the emphasis on swinging through a gate as opposed to hitting an object.

Simple tools, helpful drill.

✔ CHECKLIST
SWEETSPOT DRILL

✔ Set up the three tees as shown in the photos.

✔ Hitting only the red center tee indicates an accurate sweetspot hit.

✔ Knocking either white tee indicates an inaccurate swing plane.

✔ Verify the toe of your club points in the air as your arms reach parallel on the backswing.

✔ Verify the toe of your club points to the target on the top of your backswing.

1- FIND THE SWEETSPOT

Use a red tee to simulate the ball. Place it in the ground about halfway up the center of the clubface.

2- TOE GATE

Place a white tee just off the toe.

3- HEEL GATE

Place another white tee at an angle about an inch outside of the heel. You now have a gate to swing through. The key is to only hit the red tee.

4- SWEETSPOT IMPACT

Swinging through the gate the clubface only hit the red tee, resulting in an accurate middle iron swing. The next two photos are examples of mishits, resulting in off-target shots.

TOE HIT—BALL GOES RIGHT

On this swing the toe incorrectly hit the outside tee. Toe hits open the face of the club, sending the ball to the right.

HEEL HIT—BALL GOES LEFT

Knocking the inside tee out of the ground indicates an incorrect heel hit. This closes the clubface, sending the ball off target to the left.

M

BEHIND THE POLE DRILL

You can do this drill in your backyard without a ball or on the range with one. In both cases the drill visually encourages you to stay in position while swinging around the spine position you set properly at address.

One of the big reasons for missing shots is unnecessary body movement. Swaying back leads to fat shots. The clubface hits the ground behind the ball and then stumbles into it.

Swaying forward leads to some equally ugly shots. The club hits the ground past the ball. Accuracy requires a square clubface at impact, traveling at maximum velocity. That can only be consistently mastered by staying in position. Staying behind the pole in this drill provides the training you need.

Martin will stay on the same side of the pole throughout his swing.

1- ADDRESS BEHIND THE POLE

Position the ball opposite your left instep–the lowest point of your swing arc–and the pole is on the outside of the left foot. Stay behind the pole throughout the swing.

2- BACKSWING BEHIND THE POLE

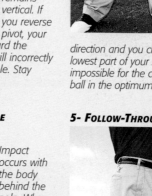

You might think staying behind the pole on the backswing is easy. It is, as long as you do not reverse pivot. Your weight goes back and your spine angle remains vertical. If you reverse pivot, your spine angle will be tilting toward the target and your upper body will incorrectly be on the other side of the pole. Stay behind the pole for accuracy!

3- DOWNSWING BEHIND THE POLE

As the butt of the club reaches the downswing power slot position for a delayed hit, you should remain correctly behind the pole. Not swaying forward is equally as important as not swaying back.

Sway in either direction and you change the position of the lowest part of your swing arc, making it impossible for the clubhead to return to the ball in the optimum position.

4- IMPACT BEHIND THE POLE

Impact occurs with the body behind the pole. When you drive a nail, you stand behind to powerfully hit it. You never stand in front because that would result in a diminished source of power and efficiency. The same thing is true with your golf swing. Stay behind the pole for accuracy and power.

5- FOLLOW-THROUGH BEHIND THE POLE

The swing finishes behind the pole. All the weight is on the left foot as evidenced by the bent position of the right leg. This is an excellent backyard drill without a ball. You can improve many aspects of your game right at home.

EYES CLOSED TEMPO/TIMING DRILL

Tempo and timing play pivotal roles in accuracy. When all the moving parts have the time to come together, accuracy is the positive result.

After closing your eyes at address, work through this drill slowly, beginning without a ball until you feel the tempo and timing taking over naturally. Then hit some balls using the same feelings you just developed.

Close your eyes to feel the correct timing and tempo.

1- ADDRESS

Address the ball with your legs close together. Close your eyes!

2- BACKSWING

Keeping your eyes closed, swing back to the top of a 9 o'clock backswing. Maintain your power triangle with the grip in front of your chest. Have someone watch and they can stop you if the toe of the club is not pointed to the sky. No sense in practicing an incorrect swing plane.

3- DOWNSWING

Swing down to the ball. Keep your eyes closed so that all of your senses are tuned to feeling the tempo.

4- ABBREVIATED FOLLOW-THROUGH

Swing through the ball. Feel the tempo and timing. Stop about halfway through on your follow-through. Notice the spine and head remained in the same position, at left.

M

NARROW FIELD OF VISION

When concentrating on a specific task, like reading a putt with your club Championship on the line or just to liberate a few dollars from your buddies on Saturday morning, it helps to limit the information you ask your brain to process. Narrowing your field of vision brings only the essential information to the forefront for the process of finding the line to the hole.

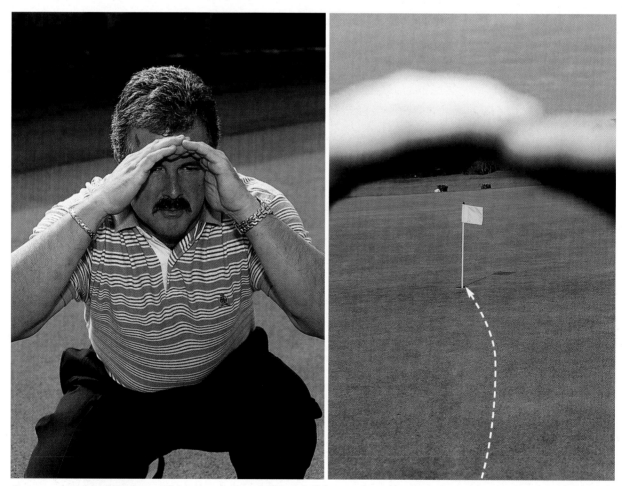

Once you have the green's overall topography in mind and feel the speed it takes to get the ball to the hole, narrow your field of vision for another look. Place your hands over your eyes, eliminating the extraneous view so you can concentrate on seeing the line to the hole. Focus on what matters.

NEW EQUIPMENT AND TECHNIQUES

Over the years Tom Lehman's game has had to evolve to accommodate revolutionary changes occurring in both club and ball technology. Unlike equipment in years gone by, today's high-tech clubs and balls are all geared to go straight, so the ball does not curve as much as it used to.

Re-adjusting aim is essential. For example, Tom used to aim 20 or 30 feet right of the hole for a draw. Today, that shrinks down to 10 or 15 feet. If you're used to hitting a 30-foot fade, that might be only a 15-foot fade today, because the ball makes it go straighter.

Tom Lehman has adapted his long game to reflect recent equipment developments.

LAUNCH ANGLE

Tom wants a low launch angle with higher ball spin.

Today, everyone is striving for the ultimate launch angle to fly the ball the maximum distance. That's great off the tee but it does a disservice to players with their irons. Hitting an iron, you should not be looking to maximize your distance; you should be looking to maximize your accuracy. It's not like you are looking to hit it as far as you can. It's more like hitting it as far as you want to.

Players who hit the ball really high off the tee can find help in the long distance balls that are engineered to launch high but spin less. But if you're a player who has always hit the ball low with more spin, these new balls are not suited to your game. They were not created to add spin, so they can't and won't react that way when you hit them.

If low trajectories with spin are your stock in trade, as they are for me, our best choice in balls is one that launches low and spins more. This cushions the air resistance a little so we can control our distances.

Because you're serious about improving your game, be very demanding when selecting balls and clubs. Just because something is currently the hottest thing on the market doesn't mean it's right for our games. I take my equipment selection seriously and you should too.

AROUND THE GREENS

Even around the greens, the new balls feel differently than the old ones. Some are harder and probably don't spin as much. That makes it harder to control your chip shots. Lots of players have had to adjust their techniques to work it all out.

Chipping and putting with the new balls feels different.

N

ORDER OF MOTION

The race engine of a Formula One Ferrari accelerates the car from 0 to 100 mph in less than five seconds. On a golf swing, the clubhead speed of a PGA TOUR professional climbs over 120 mph in less than 1.5 seconds. That's impressive, but even more so when you realize the downswing takes only a half second of the total.

The similarity between such high-performance examples of perfection is the smoothness created by following an order of motion. Just as the Ferrari would sputter and stall if the electronic onboard computers fired the sparks in the wrong order for the 10-cylinder engine, Tom Lehman's swing would share similar destruction from being out of sequence. Tune up your swing to follow the correct order of motion for permanent game improvement.

BACKSWING ORDER

There are many moving parts in the swing. The advantage of having a connected swing is that the motion of a few parts controls the motion of many. My backswing order of motion begins with the upper body taking the lead.

START TO EXTENSION

SMOOTH SWING

The upper body has a greater distance to rotate and must start in this order:

1. Shoulders, arms, hands and club.

2. Hips.

My upper body triangle moves away together. The shoulders, arms, hands and club are similar to the sides of a triangle and stay connected for this one-piece take-away. Hip movement comes next as the rotating shoulders pull them back.

The triangle moves away together.

> ### BACKSWING ORDER OF MOTION
>
> 1- Shoulders, arms, hands and club move together.
>
> 2- Hip rotation occurs as a result of being pulled by the shoulders.
>
> 3- Natural upward motion cocks the wrists.
>
> 4- Hip movement finishes.
>
> 5- Shoulders continue to wind up.

SWING MISFIRES

The rotation sequence begins incorrectly with the lower body. If you rotate your hips before your shoulders, you surrender any possibility of making a good golf swing. You can't store any power.

Nearing the Top

Smooth Swing

1. Upper body rotation continues.

2. Wrists cock naturally.

3. Lower body rotation has stopped.

My shoulders and the power triangle continue to move away from the ball. Notice the position of the hips compared to the last photo. Their rotation was limited. The wrinkles on the back and side of my shirt show the stored-up power. I'm winding up like a spring.

Winding up like a spring.

My wrists have cocked as my relaxed, tension-free grip allows the weight of the swinging clubhead to pull them into position. The backswing takes a full second, and you must relax, trusting the laws of physics to do the work. Once the correct posture angles are set at address and the correct order of motion is followed, you will be playing vastly improved golf.

Swing Misfires

The hips start first and over-rotate. The body can't wind up the power unless your hips resist their backswing rotation. The wrist cock is too early, the result of a conscious movement instead of a natural one.

Dropping the Flag

Once the body has been wound up, this position is like punching the launch control button on the Formula One Ferrari. That revolutionary onboard computer program actually takes control of the car, up-shifting through the gears while increasing the fuel to eliminate wheel spin at the start. This is very sophisticated electronics.

Transition

Smooth Swing

1. Left hip moves toward the target.

2. Left knee moves toward the target.

3. Shoulders and power triangle continue their backswing movement.

In today's electronic world, winding up toys and clocks is a lost art. But if your memory goes back that far think about what it felt like. One hand did the winding while the other provided some resistance as it steadily held the object being wound. Power was being stored, and you gave it that last little rotation to get it fully wound.

Shoulders wind up the rest of the way.

The principle of your golf swing is the same. The hips are offering the resistance as they begin the turn back toward the target while the shoulders continue winding up that extra amount. Compare this photo with the previous one and you'll see the left knee has moved toward the ball but the club is farther back. Power is peaking.

Swing Misfires

If the arms incorrectly start the transition, the clubhead will go outside the swing plane and impact the ball from an outside-to-in position. You don't have to be a physics major to recognize a weak slice when you see one.

O

DOWNSWING

DOWNSWING ORDER OF MOTION

1- Knees moving to the target.

2- Hips moving to the target.

3- Power upper body triangle moving to the target.

Now both parts of the body move toward the target. The powers of centrifugal force take over. My clubhead speed and yours can never climb as high as we are capable of by trying to swing fast. We have to sequence motion properly, allowing basic physics to take over.

ARMS PARALLEL

SMOOTH SWING

1. Hip rotation.

2. Hip rotation pulls arms down.

My power triangle did not start down by itself. It was pulled down by my lower body's rotation back to the target. I want the clubhead to follow a swing plane that brings it slightly from the inside to a square position at impact, and then return to the inside to follow-through. This order of motion makes that possible.

SWING MISFIRES

Arms begin first or hips are over-rotating. Both motions are incorrect and result in either a slice to the right or a pull to the left.

Hip rotation pulls the arms down.

POWER SLOT

SMOOTH SWING

1. Smooth hip motion.

2. Upper body power triangle moves together.

The lower body is smoothly rotating and the power triangle is rapidly gaining speed. The correct order of motion brings me to the address position with the exception of my slightly open hips, which create the room for the arms to swing through.

Power is developed when all the parts arrive at the ball together. The wrists are still cocked and are entering the power slot.

SWING MISFIRES

The wrists release prematurely and the hips are considerably open to the target line, almost facing the target. This motion spins everything out of control.

The power triangle gains speed.

IMPACT TO PAST IMPACT

Hips have cleared, wrists have not released.

SMOOTH SWING

1. Hips have cleared.

2. Power triangle was intact going through the ball.

3. Wrists have not released.

This even looks smooth in a still photo. My hip motion cleared away enough space for my power triangle to swing through, ensuring the clubhead impacted the ball squarely. My wrists did not release even at this point: power was not scrubbed off.

SWING MISFIRES

Hips that are facing the target. Wrists release prematurely, sending the clubhead ahead of the ball prior to impact.

FOLLOW-THROUGH

Wrists release.

Shoulder rotation brings head up.

SMOOTH SWING

1. Wrists have released.

2. Head rotates upward as a result of shoulder rotation.

3. Shoulders and power triangle continue to the finish.

This is the first head motion you've seen, and I didn't purposely look up; the shoulder rotation pulled it up. The hips stop first and the upper body continues to swing around to finish. The wrists released as the clubhead pulled them through. This is a natural, free-flowing swing with the correct order of motion.

SWING MISFIRES

Hips stop too early or finish too early. In either case the clubhead could not have been square to the target line at impact.

O

PITCHING

Pitches vs. Chips. Do you know the difference between them and how to adapt your short game technique to both? Flight trajectory is the key, as Tom Lehman shows you in this section. Then, once and for all, Martin Hall clears up the age-old question: *Where do you aim when the face is open?*

✔ CHECKLIST
PITCH SHOTS

✔ Determine the trajectory you need for individual short game shots. A higher trajectory that flies the ball farther onto the green is a pitch shot. Pitches are also effective the farther off the green you are.

✔ Find your putting line to the hole and choose a landing target along that line.

✔ Select a club that provides the desired loft for the flight.

✔ Adjust your stance for how much release you want after landing.

✔ Shaft is not positioned ahead of the body, as it was for a chip, because here the ball, not the run, must carry most of the distance.

Let's begin by comparing the launch trajectory of a pitch to that of a chip.

PITCH

Pitches are high.

CHIP

Chips are low.

Pitches are hit higher than chips, and each offers a strategical advantage. Chip shots (see Chipping) should just skim over the grass, landing a pace or two on the green and then rolling the rest of the way along a predetermined putting line. Pitch shots stay in the air longer, covering more green before landing.

Clubhead loft at impact is the key angle difference, even though both shots can be played with the same club. Developing shotmaking versatility with any club turns you into an expert short game player. Versatility begins at address.

ADDRESS

Using the same 56-degree wedge, let's compare pitch and chip address positions.

PITCH

CHIP

- *Ball position is in the middle of the stance.*

- *Hands are slightly ahead of the ball.*

- *Stance is open to the target line.*

This setup position encourages a more-lofted shot. The clubhead alignment will be open to my stance alignment as the swing cuts under the ball. Launching the ball on a higher trajectory allows it to carry more green prior to landing.

- *Ball position is behind the right foot for this running chip.*

- *The hands are farther ahead of the ball than they were for the pitch.*

- *Stance is open to the target line.*

This setup encourages a running shot. The club will be less lofted at impact and the ball will skim over the fringe, landing a few paces on the green and then releasing toward the hole.

ADDRESS DETAIL

For this particular pitch we'll assume the pin is in the middle of the green. Strategically, I want a pitch that lands and runs only a short distance.

As with chip shots and most shorter scoring zone shots, your stance should be open to the target line, setting up the parameters for the correct swing plane. Because the lower body remains stationary during the swing, opening the stance (arrow 1) creates room for the arms to swing the club through along the target line (arrow 2).

P

DOWNSWING

Backswing length is based on the length of the shot. In the action photo below you can see the club was taken back to hip height for this shot.

You can easily see the pitching swing arc in this action shot. Approaching correctly from the inside, it's obvious the club didn't go straight back. This avoided an all too common mistake that takes loft away from the face, causing a lower pushed shot.

IMPACT

The mark of all good golf shots, long or short, is a crisp, solid hit. Pitch shots require the same quality of impact. With a soft grip and relaxed tempo swing you should feel the ball staying on the clubface through impact. The ball rolls up lofted faces, creating slightly higher trajectories. Abrupt hits into the ball result in a rebound effect, with loss of distance control and flight dynamics.

Solid impact is vital for hitting the ball the correct distance.

FACE UP FOLLOW-THROUGH

Unlike chip shots, the pitching clubface does not stay low through the impact zone. It comes up slightly with an open face. Chip shots run almost from the start, while pitches have to fly and release.

Notice the clubhead position and the loft of the ball. A short follow-through with the face in the air is a picture-perfect pitch finish position.

PITCHING ACCURACY

Are you confused about where to aim once you open the face of a club? Let's deal with that immediately, and then I'll show you how to set up perfectly every time.

Martin Hall demonstrates the proper aiming technique for accurate pitch shots.

Tom pointed out that a common pitching error is to take the clubhead straight back instead of following the natural inside swing arc. Using a beach ball will cure you of that problem quickly.

Set up for a pitch shot with one important difference: place a beach ball between your forearms.

CLUBFACE AIMS LEFT

Aim your clubface slightly left of the target and open your stance. The correct swing should be along your foot line, and the face slips under the ball in the fully lofted position set at address.

LAY THE FACE BACK

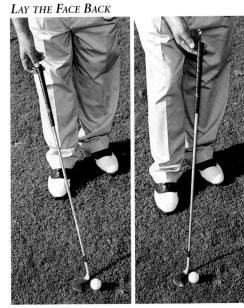

The foolproof way to open the clubface properly is to aim the club slightly left of your target and then lay the face back (left). This ensures the clubface remains square to the target line. If you try to twist it open, aligning it at address (right), chances are your aiming accuracy will suffer.

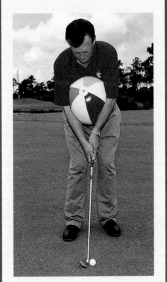

As you swing back, keep the beach ball between your arms to provide the inside arc feeling. Swinging straight back lifts a forearm and the ball will fall out.

SQUARE HIGHER TRAJECTORY LOFT SQUARE LOW TRAJECTORY LOFT

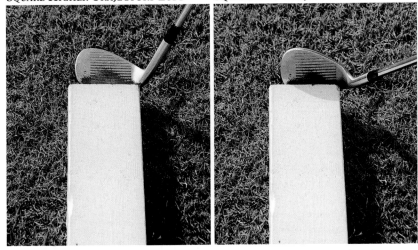

With a 2 x 4 illustrating the target line, the open, high-lofted clubhead stays as square as it was for the lower trajectory shot (left). Laying the shaft down is a foolproof way to set the loft yet keeps the clubhead square every time (right).

P

POSTURE

The angle of your spine has to be set properly at address or the rest of your swing will be one big compensation. An overstatement? Not really! A rotational swing needs a stable center.

Tom is even more emphatic about good posture (this page), and demonstrates two examples of bad posture (page 115) that destroy any chance for game improvement.

Tom's excellent posture, set at address, creates solid hits at impact.

✔ **CHECKLIST**

POSTURE

✔ Stand tall.

✔ Bend at the waist.

✔ Keep the back as straight as possible.

✔ Keep your thighs and hamstrings up so they can be strong.

✔ Chin out.

How important do I think posture is to the success of a golf swing? There is no getting around the fact that you are not able to turn as well around a spine that is curved as a spine that is straight.

The better your posture, the better you can turn. Some people misinterpret the term, "a good athletic position." Usually the example used is a quarterback taking a snap from center. If you set up to the golf ball like that, the deep knee bend makes it impossible to turn without bobbing up and down.

Using the quarterback example for good posture, visualize how they look while awaiting a shotgun snap. Balanced stance, head up, spine straight and bent waist are what you'll see.

Keep your spine straight. Wide swing arcs along the correct plane are created by the very first portion of your golf swing: the setup.

Keep your chin up. Tucking it into your chest, because someone said you need to keep your head down, limits shoulder rotation.

Arms hang naturally down in this easy-to-repeat position.

Posture is correctly set if you can draw a line from your shoulders that bisects your knees and terminates into the laces of your shoes. When you duplicate this position, swinging around a fixed angle will be much easier and consistent.

Here's what's wrong with this posture:

- *There is no spine angle. Bending is not from the waist.*

- *Bending is done incorrectly from the knees. The line from the shoulders ends up in back of the knees instead of through the kneecap.*

- *The hands are extended way out. Anytime you stand too up-and-down, your hands go out and the club rotates around too flat.*

Here's what's wrong with this posture:

- *Bent over too far.*

- *The line from the shoulders cannot even touch a knee. There is no balance point in this incorrect position.*

- *The arms are up against the thigh. There is no room to create an accurate swing plane. When the hands get this close, as a result of bending over the ball, the club gets too vertical on the backswing,*

P

PRE-SHOT ROUTINES

Pre-shot routines develop confidence in your golf swing. Doing everything in an orderly, repeatable fashion takes away stress and uncertainty. Good routines include motions to program a feel for the shot at hand. While PGA TOUR professionals' routines may differ, they share one important trait—having a pre-shot routine in the first place.

Tom Lehman's pre-shot routine begins when he gets the yardage from his caddie and determines what the wind is doing. As soon as he pulls a club from his bag, it begins for real.

1- PULL A CLUB

Tom's routine starts the instant he takes a club out of the bag.

2- VISUALIZE THE SHOT

He goes behind the ball to visualize the exact shot he wants to hit.

3- FEEL THE SWING

Taking several practice swings allows you to feel the type of shot you want to play. If it's going to be a fade, feel a fade. Programming a draw takes its own thoughts.

4- ELIMINATE TENSION

Because tension tends to build up in the shoulders and neck, stretching is part of many pre-shot routines. Maybe do a neck stretch before continuing with the routine. Tension is a swing inhibitor and the routine helps you relieve it before a problem affects the quality of your swing.

5- MOVE TO THE BALL

Time to walk up to the ball, keeping all the positive thoughts and visualizations in your mind.

6- ADDRESS

As you begin to take your stance, consider all the things we covered in this book regarding grip, posture, address, alignment and ball position.

7- WAGGLE

Tom is a five-waggle guy. The last thing he does is initiate the swing with a slight forward press and then everything begins.

PUTTING

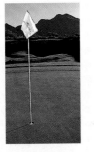

Putting strokes are as different on the PGA TOUR as they are among your friends. This is one phase of the game where individuality triumphs, as long as two criteria are met.

- The putter face impacts the ball square to the line the putt starts off on.

- The putt's speed has been factored in when selecting the correct line to the hole.

Tom has some professional insight into his putting approach, and then comments on the styles of a few of the TOUR's best putters. Martin Hall has a few drills to help sharpen your putting skills.

✔ CHECKLIST
PUTTING

✔ Select a putter that feels good and has the correct loft and lie for your game.

✔ Get comfortable in your stance.

✔ Do not change your grip pressure during your stroke.

✔ Keep wrists firm throughout the stroke.

✔ Strive for a constant, rhythmic swing.

✔ Point the butt of your putter at a certain spot throughout your swing.

TOM'S PUTTING STROKE

To demonstrate the important aspects of putting, I'm not using a ball. All too often mistakes are made by being so "hit the ball" oriented that you forget the important elements of the swing. Let's begin with a balanced grip.

TOM'S GRIP   *PALMS FACING PALMS*

This is a balanced grip that could help you square the putter face at contact.

Notice how the palms face one another before and after closing the grip. During the stroke, grip pressure does not change.

PENDULUM STROKE

Notice how the butt of the putter always points to the sternum during this rhythmic stroke. The putter goes back and through on a constant plane.

The putter goes back and releases through, as opposed to dragging the handle one way or the other. That means the putter head is being swung through the stroke instead of being manipulated.

The stroke's speed remains constant. You don't want to decelerate or accelerate. Feel a constant speed, with the butt pointed at your sternum, and let the pendulum take over.

P

Tom's TOUR Analyses

Dave Stockton

Simultaneous forward press and movement back.

Dave is one of the best putters ever, and players on both the PGA TOUR and SENIOR TOUR seek his advice. Stockton's take-away is unique because of a simultaneous forward press with his hands as the blade goes back.

This is one movement, not two separate ones. Dave's putter is ideal for his stroke. While most putters have three degrees of loft, Dave's has five degrees due to his forward press and take-away. Using a three-degree putter would create negative loft, driving the ball into the ground at contact.

Jim Furyk

Cross-handed grip keeps wrists firm.

Jim Furyk has always used a cross-handed putting grip because of a conversation his teaching pro father had with Arnold Palmer and Gary Player while Jim was growing up in Pennsylvania.

Both said they would be cross-handed putters if they were starting their careers over. The reason: cross-handed grips help keep the wrists from breaking down during the stroke. Firm wrists are important to a good stroke.

Two-time U.S. Open champion Lee Janzen takes his putter back on an inside stroke arc.

Jim also takes the clubhead back straight behind the ball. Other players, like Lee Janzen, prefer a slightly inside swing arc. Compare the two.

Lee Janzen

Controlled backswing, great rhythm.

Lee Janzen's putting stroke is very similar to his long game swing. Both feature an in-control backswing.

Lee's putting philosophy is different than mine. I prefer to keep my pendulum stroke in motion while he prefers to:

1 Take the club back under control.

2 Pause slightly.

3 Putt through.

His rhythm obviously works extremely well for him. Lee's triangle in the photo is another reason for his putting expertise. His shoulders stay parallel to the target line but move as a unit with the arms.

MARTIN'S SQUARE FACE CONTACT DRILL

Bringing a square face back to the ball is essential for good putting. This drill helps you practice putting perfection.

DRILL SETUP

Place a tee by the heel and toe of your putter, with the ball positioned in the center of the blade. This is not a gate to stroke through; you want to knock both tees simultaneously.

Stroke back and forth. Here's your report card:

- *Both tees knocked down (bottom photo) = a square clubface.*
- *Heel tee knocked down first = open clubface at impact.*
- *Toe tee knocked down first = closed clubface at impact.*

RHYTHM DRILL

This drill helps establish a feeling for backstrokes and follow-throughs of equal length.

RHYTHM DRILL

Place two angled shafts in the ground at equal distances behind and in front of the ball. They should be slightly behind the target line because of the inside-to-inside stroke arc.

Stroke back (left) and through (right), tapping each so that the sounds appear equal: Tap. Tap. Try this first without a ball to develop consistent rhythm.

P

QUESTIONABLE LIES

During every round, situations arise prompting the question: How should I play a shot when several alternatives are possible? Take the case of finding your ball close to the green but situated against the collar of the second cut of rough. With higher grass behind it, shorter grass in front of it and about two yards before the green begins, you have some decisions to make.

Once you get close to the green, strokes must be saved, not squandered. You do not want to waste this scoring opportunity. Deciding whether to chip or putt is only the peripheral choice. Some creative adaptations—utilizing clubs designed for other purposes—are also in the equation. So what should you do? Martin Hall demonstrates some potential answers.

AGAINST THE COLLAR

For whatever reason, your approach shot rolled through the green and came to rest against the collar of the second rough. Take consolation that at least part of it remains on some shorter grass instead of burying itself in the longer stuff so close to the green. You can play this shot successfully, getting it close or even in, once you understand some potential problems.

1 The back of the ball is against the longer grass, which can become trapped between the clubface and ball at impact and make distance control difficult.

2 The longer grass can grab the clubface before impact, slightly twisting it, which sends the ball off line.

3 After impact, the ball is still on the first cut of rough. Decide if you want the ball to roll through it or fly over it. The hardness of the green and other conditions help make that decision for you.

With the ball resting against the collar, golfers have several choices on how to best play the shot.

SOLUTIONS TO THE QUESTION

After assessing the situation, finding the line to the hole and determining the green and collar condition, here are your three basic choices:

1 Chip the ball and hope to control both accuracy and distance. Maybe the taller grass getting trapped between ball and clubhead won't make that much difference.

2 Putt the ball and hope to roll it over the fringe onto the green. Forget about the tall grass the putter will have to transverse back and through.

3 Play the shot successfully like a pro. This is the obvious choice and the one I'll demonstrate.

PROS' CHOICES

These are the guys who score low for a living, so let's take a look at four choices they work with to play this shot successfully. If you want to learn, learn from the best! Here are the methods:

1 Pop the ball with a descending putter to avoid the tall grass grabbing the club.

2 Blade the ball with a sand wedge instead of chipping it.

3 Putt the ball with a 3-wood, a club the ground can't catch.

4 Putt the ball with the toe of the putter.

#1. POP IT WITH A PUTTER

The ground in front of the ball has to be firm for this technique to work successfully. To get the ball to pop out and over the fringe, the ground acts as a backboard to bounce the ball off of, so firmness is needed.

A putter's descending blow pops the ball away from the collar, flying it over the fringe.

1- DESCENDING BLOW SETUP

Play the ball back in your stance. Notice it's several inches outside of the right foot. The negative loft on the putter face is established by the hands' forward position.

2- BACKSWING

Abruptly pick up the clubhead.

3- ANGLE OF ATTACK

Far from a level putting stroke, this sharper downward angle of attack avoids the grass all the way to impact. You want the ball to pop out and over instead of rolling.

4- POP

After popping the ball against the firm ground, causing it to jump into the air, the putter head comes to rest in the ball's previous position. Had the ground been soft, it would have forced the ball into the ground instead of popping it up and over.

Q

#2. BLADE IT WITH YOUR SAND WEDGE

Your sand wedge is designed for loft and also propelling a sand cushion to extricate a ball from the bunker. This shot adapts it for a hybrid mixture of chipping and putting.

Developed to avoid trapping the longer grass between the clubface and ball, this is the only time when blading the shot is the desired result. Another advantage is avoiding a grass-twisted clubhead at impact. Even a marginal twisting results in an off-line shot.

Blading the ball takes the longer grass out of play.

Position the ball opposite your left heel. Use a putting grip. Keep your posture upright.

2- BACKSWING

A level putting backswing takes the sand wedge away from the ball. Notice how the clubhead avoids the grass going back.

3- DOWNSTROKE

The sand wedge's built-in loft will not come into play at impact. This level putting stroke return to the ball allows the heavy portion of the clubhead to make contact around the middle without trapping the grass. Striking the ball at the equator allows the clubhead mass to do all the work.

4- IMPACT

After blading the ball's equator it stays low, skimming over the fringe.

#3. PUTT WITH A 3-WOOD

Although closely identified with Tiger Woods, this shot has been around for decades. It just goes to show that even the best players can learn a trick or two from the past. In this case, a 3-wood, with the design capability to produce 200 plus yard shots, is adapted for putting!

1- CHOKE DOWN

Addressing the ball using a 3-wood with a putting stance necessitates choking down on the club to position it more upright. Grip it the same way you grip your putter. Notice that palms are facing before the grip is closed.

2- FORWARD STROKE

After a level-putting backstroke, the wood returns to the ball along a similarly level approach. Three-woods will not get twisted in the grass, twisting the face off line.

3- IMPACT

After a level hit, the ball rolls over the fringe. The toe impact and using a putting stroke control the distance.

4- FOLLOW-THROUGH LOW

A putting follow-through is level as is this one. Notice the clubhead only leaves the ground by a few inches. The ball will roll over the fringe and onto the green. Practicing the feel to control your distances is highly recommended.

THE SWEETSPOT IS THE TOE

If your choice for this shot is putting with a 3-wood, the key to success is using the toe of the club instead of the full face. Raising the heel off the ground begins the process.

FACE = LONG GAME   TOE = PUTTING

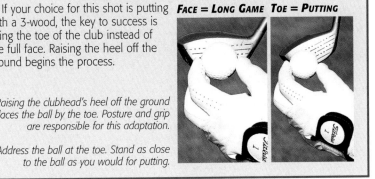

Raising the clubhead's heel off the ground places the ball by the toe. Posture and grip are responsible for this adaptation.

Address the ball at the toe. Stand as close to the ball as you would for putting.

#4. PUTTING TOE HIT

The most difficult of the four options is striking the ball with the putter's toe. The late Payne Stewart used this shot with great success, but it takes a lot of practice. Rocco Mediate also uses this technique for special situations.

1- ADDRESS

Rocco uses a long putter and his address is normal except for pointing the toe toward the target (inset). Be sure the clubface is aimed at the center of the ball.

2- STROKE

Staying on the stroke plane is paramount to hitting the center of the ball with the putter's toe. A pendulum motion helps. The length of the stroke takes care of the distance.

The advantage to this shot: It limits the amount of the putter head that can be affected by the grass. The ball will pop up before rolling over the remaining fringe.

Q

R

REVERSE SHOT

PGA TOUR professionals are not immune from getting into trouble. Even the best planned shot executed by a world-class player can go astray, requiring creativity to extricate it from an almost hopeless situation.

Perhaps no more creative shot exists than the reverse shot, where a right-handed player has to become a lefty to get his ball back into position. However, not having a set of left-handed clubs in the bag further complicates the matter. That's where creativity comes into play.

Right-handed Skip Kendall has to play this reverse shot like lefties Phil Mickelson and Mike Weir.

STAY IN CONTROL

All good swings, even those played from the opposite side, have common elements to success. Skip Kendall plays this opposite wedge shot maintaining the good fundamentals seen in his normal golf swing.

The triangle formed by the lines connecting his shoulders, arms and hands can be seen in the photo. When this occurs, the grip portion of his club can stay in front of the chest. That's extremely important for all shots. It ensures that the clubface is square at impact, but is especially true for this shot with only an inverted clubface to work with.

IMPACT AND FOLLOW-THROUGH

Skip, like all PGA TOUR players, practices various shots just in case he needs them, and always has his objectives for the shot clear in his mind prior to stepping in. In this case, just getting the ball back in the fairway is his only intention. Positive mental preparation, along with practiced fundamentals, reinforces Skip's total commitment to the shot.

Staying in control, by slowing down his swing, encourages the solid contact needed to get the ball back in the fairway for his next shot. Notice how Skip has adhered to another basic fundamental: His head has remained in place.

R

ROUGH

Playing a ball from the rough requires some modification from playing the shot from the fairway. With the deeper grass jailing your ball, trying to grab your clubhead and twisting it off the target line, accommodations must be made.

Successful shots from the rough are attributable to modifying your shotmaking technique to combat the taller grass.

✔ CHECKLIST
DEEPER ROUGH

✔ Play the ball so it runs after landing.

✔ Close the clubface before gripping, and play the ball back in your stance and aim left of your target.

✔ Swinging steeper to the ball limits "grab" from the taller grass.

✔ Accelerate through impact.

✔ Make a complete follow-through.

CLOSE THE CLUBFACE

The first change from your normal technique is to slightly close the clubface **before gripping the club.** This simple change helps keep the shot on line by resisting the grass twisting the clubhead open prior to impact. **Compensate for this adjustment by aiming left of your target.**

TOM'S DEFINITION

FLYER

A flyer is when tall grass catches the club and also gets between the face and the ball. The grooves can't grip the ball to apply backspin. Without backspin the ball will fly lower and hotter, running a longer distance after landing. Take that into consideration when selecting a landing target, and adjust your club choice accordingly.

STEEPER SWING

The tracking lines of his hands and clubhead illustrate Scott Hoch's steeper swing plane when in the rough.

Scott Hoch became a master of playing out of the rough early in his career, before improvements in his driving accuracy made that situation a less common occurrence. He found that a steeper swing through thicker lies lessens the effect the taller grass has on the clubhead.

A normal swing exposes the clubhead to the longer grass for an increased period of time, allowing it to grab the face open. Sideways or baffled and weak shots will be the result. The steeper swing eliminates, or at least lessens, that problem.

ACCELERATE

This golf swing needs to be smooth but aggressive. Quitting on the shot when you begin to feel the resistance from the grass will doom it. The key is to be smooth but make sure you accelerate the swing through the impact zone. Try these tips:

• Before addressing the ball, program your mind to expect a different feeling on the downswing.

• Make three practice swings.

• Everything should be smooth but increase the acceleration through the impact zone with each swing.

• Make sure you finish in a complete follow-through position with each practice swing.

• Only when you are pre-programmed for this feeling can you confidently step in and be totally committed to the shot.

Complete your follow-through.

FOLLOW-THROUGH

Scott finished the shot in a complete follow-through position. One of the major causes of rough breakdown is failing to accelerate through the ball. Your pre-shot practice swings should include finishing like Scott to pre-program you to swing for success.

Accelerate through the shot.

MARTIN'S SHOTMAKING TIPS

ADJUST BEFORE GRIPPING

When you adjust the clubface open or closed, make sure you grip the club only after you have made the change. This is the surefire way for re-creating this position at impact.

Gripping and then turning the face open or shut is a huge mistake, as you can never hold that adjustment throughout your swing. So remember to adjust before gripping!

R

RUN-UP SHOT

Controlling ball trajectory and spin are the hallmarks of a good golfer. Great results are attributable only to understanding and mastering advanced techniques. Golf is a game of angles combined with physics, but only a few adjustments have to be made before allowing the club to do its job.

Run-up shots can be employed in a variety of situations but the most common is a short approach shot.

SENIOR PGA TOUR professional Chi Chi Rodriguez controls the ball's trajectory for a lower bump-and-run shot.

✔CHECKLIST
RUN-UP SHOTS

✔ Pick out an interim landing target along the path to the hole.

✔ Select a less-lofted club (an 8-iron instead of a wedge, for example).

✔ Position the ball back in your stance, and choke down on the grip.

✔ Use a shoulder swing.

✔ Match follow-through length to backswing length.

SHOULDER SWING

Your shoulders direct the run-up shot. They do all the work while a passive lower body provides a steady base. These photos of Chi Chi Rodriguez, a short-game wizard, demonstrate how he returned to his address position at impact with this shoulder-dominated swing. Notice he does break his wrists on the backswing. The lower body rotates only slightly to accommodate the club staying on plane as his hands lead the clubhead through the ball.

Chi Chi Rodriguez, seen taking one last look at his interim target, will replicate this address position at impact.

Impact looks just like address!

LENGTH CONTROL

A key to controlling the length of your run-up shots is to make sure your backswing and follow-through are mirror images of each other. This balanced length ensures that the clubhead will come through the ball with the proper velocity to land on your interim target.

Try these tips for run-up success:

- Visualize the ball landing on your interim target and then running up and going into the hole.

- Feel the clubhead speed it will take to reach the interim landing target.

- Make several mirror-image practice swings, visualizing the ball's velocity and trajectory to the hole.

- Relax.

- Address the shot with your mind programmed for success.

SAND PLAY

Bunkers are hazards. But for professional golfers like Tom Lehman, they pose no threat at all. In fact low handicap golfers and PGA TOUR players may even prefer to spin shots out of a bunker than be faced with an unpredictable tight lie in the fairway.

If you're thinking that sand consistency isn't exactly predictable, think again. It is, after you understand what it's telling you. Sharpen your sand shotmaking skills with Tom and Martin.

TOM'S SHOTMAKING TIPS

QUICK CONSISTENCY RULE OF THUMB

Wet sand = Take a steeper angle of approach.

Fluffy sand = Take a shallow swing using a club with a lot of built-in bounce, such as a sand wedge.

SAND STRATEGY

THINK AS YOU WALK

Tom legally tests the consistency of the sand as he walks toward his ball. Feel the sand as you walk. Is it hard, fluffy or wet? Your feet will tell you.

Sand firmness is a very big factor. The Rules of Golf obviously do not let you go into the bunker and touch it with your hands or kick it with your feet. But you can walk in it. Use your feet to feel and sense what the sand is like. You cannot test the sand, or do anything to determine how hard or soft it is. You can just walk on it. As you walk, pay attention to what it feels like. Do the same as you dig your feet in for the stance. Feel the consistency. That tells you how to play the shot.

FEEL

As you dig in, taking your stance, feel the sand. In this case, it's a little wet and heavy.

S

HARD SAND

Hard sand is easier to hit out of. I find the best way is a little steeper angle of approach to the ball, to get it to come out properly. With wet sand or hard sand if you lay the blade open and take a horizontal swing, the blade comes at the ball with a shallow angle. The bounce of the club causes it to rebound off the sand and into the ball, skulling it across the green. The keys to consistently playing this shot are:

1 Get steeper, returning more vertical to the ball.

2 Always follow through to create acceleration through the ball.

VERTICAL SWING

Tom's backswing is more vertical (up and down) to create a steeper attack angle into the ball.

STEEPER IMPACT

Allow the clubhead loft to do most of the work. This sand is hard. A steeper angle propels the ball out of the bunker.

FOLLOW-THROUGH

Always accelerate through your sand shots. Program follow-through into your mind before you play the shot. This ensures proper acceleration through the ball. Never quit too early!

FLUFFY SAND

Instructor Martin Hall believes you struggle in the softer sand by taking too much of it instead of not enough. Thinking it requires a *blast shot* to get it out, the common mistake is hitting too far behind the ball. This drill helps correct that problem.

DRILL

SOFTER SAND DRILL

Sand propels the ball out of the bunker but here are two things you **do not** want to happen when faced with this shot and one thing you **do** want to happen:

- You **do not** want to hit the shot too thin and have the blade impact the ball. That skulls the shot, causing it to hit the bunker face or fly across the green.

- You **do not** want to hit too far behind the ball and smother the clubhead speed in the sand.

- You **do** want to enter the sand at a correct distance behind the ball. This creates the sand cushion needed to propel it out.

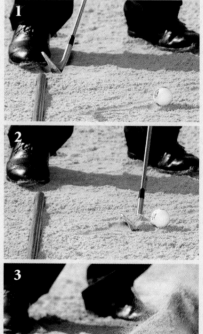

Begin your practice by placing the ball the length of your grip away from a rake handle placed in the bunker. The point of this drill is to swing your clubhead down so that it clears the rake before entering the sand.

The clubhead angle of attack misses the rake (1), impacting the sand the proper distance behind the ball (2). The perfect amount of sand cushion forms, propelling the ball out of the bunker (3) as the club follows through.

Once your consistency improves, try entering closer and closer to the ball to increase the amount of spin. Rhythmic, accelerating swings provide the control needed instead of the chaotic blasting swing seen all too often.

TOM'S SHOTMAKING TIPS

FLUFFY SAND AND BOUNCE

Fluffy sand needs a shallow swing but you'll need bounce in the club. The sand wedge has 12 degrees of bounce built into it. Without bounce a club digs in too much, losing all its speed as it digs into the sand. As a result the ball may go about 5 feet, a bad result.

You need a lot of bounce so your club can move through the sand instead of digging into it. Bounce lets the ball come out like you want it to.

SHAPING SHOTS

Having the ability to bend the ball flight to your specific needs is a necessity for playing high-level golf. High handicappers bend the ball too; the problem is they can't help it. Slices and hooks are the unfortunate examples, although sometimes you may need to create that exact ball flight on purpose.

Tom and Martin provide the help you need for understanding and then controlling shaped shots.

Tom fades the ball up and around the tree.

FADES

DOWNSWING AND IMPACT NOTES

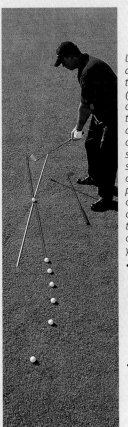

Using some dowels as teaching aids (the white one being the target line and the red ones the stance and swing path), aim your pre-opened clubface down the target line and open your stance.

- Here on the downswing, swing along the red line, parallel to your stance line.
- The face will be open and cut across the ball at impact.

Delay the rotation of the clubhead after impact. Fade sidespin (left to right) is applied to the ball.

1- THUMB

Position your left thumb on the left side of the shaft.

2- CLUBHEAD

Before taking the grip, open the clubface. By starting out with it open prior to gripping the club, no compensations will be needed to bring the clubface back to the ball in the same open position as at setup.

S

Compare these swing action photos with those on downswing and impact. The tree is the target line. At this swing checkpoint, notice how Tom's feet are open and the clubhead is pointing left of the tree. Remember: Swing along your foot line so it points in that direction. The pre-set open face will swing back to the ball and cut under it through impact.

4- Hold the Rotation

Notice that after swinging down the foot line you should hold on to the club. Don't let your right forearm come up and over the left. Follow-through positions do not create fade but they are indicative that a correct swing path was achieved to apply fade spin through impact. A similar position is a ping-pong follow-through as you cut under the ball.

Draw Follow-Through

Compare this fade follow-through with the draw follow-through (inset).

DRAWS

1- THUMB

For draws, position the left thumb on the right side of the shaft. Pre-setting this grip position makes it possible to return with it in the same position at impact.

2- CLOSE CLUBFACE

Do things the easy way and either open or close your clubface prior to setup. This makes returning to that same position at impact almost a certainty.

DOWNSWING AND IMPACT NOTES

Swing along a line parallel to your feet. At address, position the closed clubface facing the white target line and close your stance. Return to the ball along an inside-to-outside swing path.

Notice how the clubhead comes through the impact zone closed to the target line. This places draw sidespin (right to left) on the ball.

3- DRAW SETUP

With the tree as the target here, aim the pre-set clubface directly at it. close your stance.

4- DOWNSWING

Notice how the clubhead is approaching the ball from an inside to outside swing path and along the same line as the feet. At impact it will be closed to the target line, creating right-to-left spin and a draw.

5- DRAW FOLLOW-THROUGH

FADE FOLLOW-THROUGH

Compare this follow-through position (allows forearm rotation) with the fade follow-through (inset, where you hold on to delay it).

6- THE SHOT

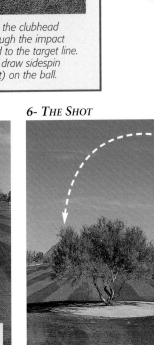

Draws move from right to left.

S

SHOULDER POSITIONS

Everyone should have a swing thought that works. It may be as simple as Scott McCarron's positive thought about trusting his swing, or maybe it's *back to the target*. We will stick with that one for this section because it's a positive thought keying a big shoulder turn. Along with Tom's demonstration of shoulder angles, you will also find information on where your shoulders should be relative to the ball, for controlling your flight trajectories.

His back is to the target, thanks to Tom's big shoulder turn.

SHOULDERS: FULL SWING

Let's begin by showing the most common example of misaligned shoulders. It's not done intentionally by most golfers. But it insidiously sneaks in as the result of checking the target one last time before initiating the swing.

✔CHECKLIST
SHOULDER POSITION

✔ Shoulders should be parallel to the target line at address.

✔ Point shoulders past the target line at the top of the backswing, with your back facing the target.

✔ Pull shoulders into the downswing with your hips.

✔ Shoulders should be parallel to the target line at impact.

✔ Point shoulders to the target line at follow-through, with your chest facing the target.

ACCIDENTAL MISALIGNMENT

We all take one final look at the target before starting the swing. The question is *how* we do it. This golfer, like many higher handicappers, unknowingly and mistakenly raised his head up to look.

In doing so he changed his shoulder position to one that is now open to the target line and in the *inadvertent slice position*. With the open knees, he will scratch his head wondering why he sliced after setting up parallel to the ball.

Setup is one thing. But you must retain that parallel position as the swing begins.

ROTATE CHIN UP

The SENIOR PGA TOUR's Bob Murphy—like all professionals—checks his target by rotating his chin up, retaining his parallel-to-the-target-line shoulder alignment. Guard against even the slightest movement that can take you out of your correct posture.

ADDRESS

PARALLEL SHOULDERS

Tom sets up his shoulders parallel to his target line. Even with a big shoulder turn, he will return them to this parallel-to-the-target position at impact.

TOP OF BACKSWING

POINT TO THE LINE

At the top of Tom's backswing, a big shoulder turn is very evident. Parallel to the line at address, the rotation away from the ball now has the shoulders pointing past the target line, and the back now faces the target.

PRE-IMPACT

ALMOST PARALLEL

As centrifugal force whirls the clubhead through the swing, the shoulders are almost parallel. As the power triangle (shoulders, arms and hands) brings the club to impact, the shoulders will return to their parallel address setup.

IMPACT ZONE

PARALLEL

Entering the impact zone, the shoulders are parallel when the club is a fraction of a second from impact. This is the delayed hit position. The club has additional distance to go, and will pick up even more speed prior to impact.

FOLLOW-THROUGH

POINTED PAST THE TARGET LINE

Finish the swing with your chest facing the target. The shoulders mirror their top-of-the-backswing position (arrow), pointing past the target line.

S

SHOULDERS: BALL FLIGHT TRAJECTORIES

HIGH FLIGHT/BEHIND THE BALL

Frank Lickliter plays his high shots with his shoulders lined up behind the ball at the top of his backswing. A forward ball position makes this possible. A swing tip: As you swing back, feel your shoulders moving behind the ball.

LOW FLIGHT IRONS/AHEAD OF THE BALL

A ball position back in the stance allows Frank to wind up his shoulders, pointing them ahead of the ball as he reaches the top. This position closes down the loft of the club at impact and creates a lower flying shot. A swing tip: Do not turn back as far as you would for a normal shot.

SHOULDERS: PUTTING

I'm a pendulum style putter, something I recommend for your immediate improvement. With the butt of the putter pointed at my sternum for the entire swing, the shoulders provide the stroke motion.

PENDULUM MOTION

Left shoulder down on the backstroke. Right shoulder down on the forward stroke.

MINI-SWING

During the stroke, the putter head does follow an arc. As a result there is an almost imperceptible shoulder rotation relative to the putting line. Here, two-time U. S. Open Champion Lee Janzen is shown from above.

BACKSTROKE

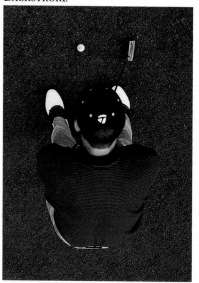

IMPACT

There is only the slightest rotation as Lee strokes his putt in these two photos. He looks parallel to the line on the backstroke (left), even though the club is following an arc. But remember the laws of physics: The farther away from the center of the motion you go, the greater the angle. In this case the shoulders are the center and their almost imperceptible rotation develops the inside arc. At impact (right), Lee's shoulders return to the true parallel position.

SHORT IRON SHOTMAKING TIPS

Shorter irons are just that: They are shorter than long irons. Along with the wedges, the category includes 8- and 9-irons. Their shorter length and increased loft requires special considerations if you want to play them effectively. Tom shows you how to get the most from these potent scoring clubs.

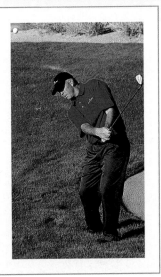

MORE VERTICAL SWING PLANE

Compare the two photos of my backswing. The short iron swing is more vertical than the long game swing. As a result of standing closer to the ball with a shorter club, the swing arc will be more up and down. But the arc should still follow the same slightly-inside-to-square to slightly-inside downswing combination of the long game swing.

The short iron swing (left) should be more vertical than the long game swing (right).

SHORT IRON BACKSWING   *DRIVER BACKSWING*

✔ CHECKLIST
SHORT IRONS

✔ Because you stand closer, the swing plane will be more vertical than for the long game.

✔ Open your stance slightly. This limits your backswing length: The club is used more for accuracy than for distance.

✔ Maintain a steady head through impact until shoulder rotation pulls the head along.

✔ Finish high for high shots and low for lower shots.

✔ Slow down your swing rhythm.

BAD SWING PLANES

Don't laugh at these swing positions. It's amazing how many times I see them in my amateur partners' swings during the course of a year. One is too steep while the other is too shallow.

TOO SHALLOW BACKSWING   *TOO STEEP BACKSWING*

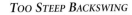

Avoid these two short iron backswing mistakes—too shallow (left), too vertical (right). See Martin's shotmaking tip on page 138 too.

S

Past impact, your head should remain in position as the fixed axis of your swing. It will only rotate up when the shoulders pull it up. Any movement up or down or back and forth causes you to hit the ball fat or thin instead of solidly.

MARTIN'S SHOTMAKING TIPS

THE BUTT OF THE CLUB

All too often we become overly focused on *hitting the ball* instead of *swinging through the ball*. Instead of concentrating on the clubhead, try checking the butt of the club, an indicator for shaft positions, at various points in your swing.

In the photos at the bottom of page 137, Tom has a wooden dowel inserted into the grip hole for illustration purposes. You can buy smaller ones like this in home-improvement or hobby stores, or just insert a tee in the hole as a pointing device. When you practice, check on what your shaft is doing as correct shaft positions automatically position the clubhead correctly.

SWING PLANE

The powers of centrifugal force take over, propelling the clubhead along a wide extended swing arc that goes up and around on the backswing, then down and around on the downswing to follow-through.

Having a clear image of what the correct swing plane looks like will help develop one of your own. These two photos of Scott Hoch, taken as the early morning dew flew off his club, provide the perfect mental image.

BACKSWING PLANE

Dew traces the backswing's swing plane.

DOWNSWING PLANE

Water flying off the club shows the power of centrifugal force.

TAKE-AWAY
ONE-PIECE TAKE-AWAY

This is the moment of truth. It's time to coordinate the movement of many independent parts into a smooth one-piece motion. If you begin with a good grip, correct address and one-piece take-away, you are well on your way to having a good, repeating golf swing. Many of your faults will be corrected as a result of mastering the first three basic fundamentals of good golf shaded in blue below.

Although they are explained in the F section, here is a brief synopsis of the basic five.

Tom Lehman begins his golf swing with a one-piece take-away.

✔CHECKLIST
FIVE BASIC FUNDAMENTALS

✔ **Grip.** Hold the club correctly.

✔ **Address.** Posture, alignment and ball position must be sound.

✔ **Take-away.** Path the club and arms take during the start of the swing is key.

✔ **Steady Head Position.** Maintains the original relationship to the ball formed at address.

✔ **Acceleration Sequencing.** The clubhead should smoothly increase speed throughout the swing.

T

TOM LEHMAN'S ONE-PIECE TAKE-AWAY: ADDRESS

Breaking down the various elements of my one-piece take-away should begin with the address position. If the definition of take-away is the path the club and arms take during the start of the swing, this position is the foundation it all builds on.

HEAD

My head and spine will be the center, or apex, of the swing. Both my backswing and downswing will revolve around this fixed point. Any movement—up, down, swaying left or right—would make it impossible for me to return to the ball at impact in this same position.

SHOULDERS

The shoulders are not level at address for this long game swing. The ball position and posture naturally make the right shoulder lower than the left. The line drawn across my chest connecting both shoulders begins the formation of a triangle. The other two sides will run down my arms. My shoulders are aligned parallel to the target line.

ARMS

My arms hang down naturally. As I grip the club, the arms form the remaining two sides of the triangle that will be maintained throughout my entire swing. The arms will bend but the appearance of the triangle remains.

HANDS

I'm gripping the club correctly, and my square-to-the-ball clubface can return back to that key position at impact.

HIPS

The hips are aligned parallel to the target line. As the take-away begins with the upper body, the hips will resist rotating back.

SLICERS' ALERT

If you tend to slice the ball, check the alignment of your shoulders at address after checking your target. A common mistake is to inadvertently move your shoulders slightly to the left if you raised your head up to look. If your shoulders remain in that position—open to the target line—you will slice the ball even if all your other fundamentals are correct.

ONE-PIECE TAKE-AWAY BEGINS

The one-piece take-away refers to the shoulders, arms, hands and club all moving away from the ball at the same time. Notice hips were not mentioned. In golf, timing is everything, and the upper body has farther to go as it winds up so it must begin moving first. If the hips lead the way you can't build torque. When they resist, as the upper body moves away from the ball, power is being stored like a tightly wound spring.

HEAD

The head has stayed steady in this part of the swing. This defines the swing's maximum extension from a fixed axis.

ARMS

Notice how the triangle, set at address, has remained as a result of the one-piece take-away. It will continue all the way to the top of my backswing. This good extension is creating a wide swing arc and coordination of all the muscles into this golf swing.

HIPS

As the club moved back together with the shoulders, arms and hands, my hips are resisting turning. They will shortly begin some rotation but will provide an element of resistance to increase the torque.

SHOULDERS

The shoulders initiated the swing along with the arms, hands and club. Notice how the rotation has brought them to a level position.

HANDS

My wrists have stayed passive and have not set the club too early in the swing. The downswing's timing will be easily coordinated because the triangle will be maintained. Power and accuracy will result from this easy-to-duplicate take-away.

LEGS

Weight transfer is beginning. Continuing the backswing, I will feel the weight almost totally over my right instep. Remember that weight follows the clubhead—away from the target on the backswing, toward the target on the downswing and follow-through.

SWING ARC

Notice the amount of distance the clubhead has already traveled (dotted line) even though the upper body has just begun rotating. The element of big circle/little circle is beginning to show, which will generate centrifugal, power-producing force on the downswing. The body rotates in a small circle while the clubhead follows a wider one.

T

ONE-PIECE MOVEMENT ACTION

BOB MURPHY'S TAKE-AWAY SWING THOUGHT

PUSH THE BAR AWAY

SENIOR PGA TOUR professional Bob Murphy suggests visualizing a bar attached to the left shoulder that continues down the shaft to the middle of the clubhead. With the shoulders, arms, hands and club "welded together" everything stays intact. To start the swing, push the left shoulder away and the rest of the parts move with it.

This combined action photo shows the linkage of Tom's one-piece take-away. He moved the club away from the ball with a connected motion created by the shoulders, arms and hands. Notice how steady his head is and how little his hips move.

TIMING AND TEMPO

Timing is the sequence of events that brings the clubhead back to the ball. Tempo is the speed of the swing. You can have a slow, natural tempo like Ernie Els or a fast tempo like Nick Price. Both work equally well as long as the timing coordinates the various movements of the swing correctly.

Tom Lehman and Martin Hall demonstrate some drills to help develop good timing and tempo.

DRILL

TEMPO ARM GRIP DRILL

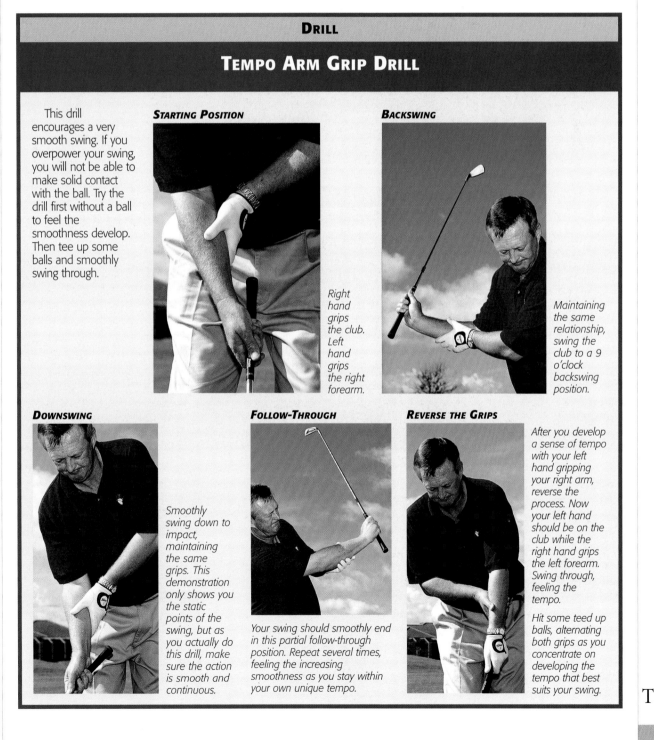

This drill encourages a very smooth swing. If you overpower your swing, you will not be able to make solid contact with the ball. Try the drill first without a ball to feel the smoothness develop. Then tee up some balls and smoothly swing through.

STARTING POSITION

Right hand grips the club. Left hand grips the right forearm.

BACKSWING

Maintaining the same relationship, swing the club to a 9 o'clock backswing position.

DOWNSWING

Smoothly swing down to impact, maintaining the same grips. This demonstration only shows you the static points of the swing, but as you actually do this drill, make sure the action is smooth and continuous.

FOLLOW-THROUGH

Your swing should smoothly end in this partial follow-through position. Repeat several times, feeling the increasing smoothness as you stay within your own unique tempo.

REVERSE THE GRIPS

After you develop a sense of tempo with your left hand gripping your right arm, reverse the process. Now your left hand should be on the club while the right hand grips the left forearm. Swing through, feeling the tempo.

Hit some teed up balls, alternating both grips as you concentrate on developing the tempo that best suits your swing.

T

THE PITCHING DRILL

Watching a baseball pitcher in slow motion is a good mental image of what timing is all about. His motions are brought together in a sequence that winds up storing power and then releases it, propelling the ball to the plate. With a motion like mine I'm surprised the Arizona Diamondbacks haven't called. A golf swing shares the same principles of timing.

For a pitcher to develop the velocity needed to blow the ball past a batter he must wind up, storing the energy on the side away from the target (Tom's right side). The transition back to the target begins with the lower body, just as it does in a golf swing. As the lower body leads the way back and the weight transfers toward the target, power is being released.

A pitcher's wrist does not release its angle before the ball leaves his hand, and neither do Tom's wrists release before impact. The ball is released at the optimum moment, when all the timing comes together. Follow through completely, as we do in our golf swings.

STEP DRILL

This drill helps you develop a sense of rhythm in your swing. You can even practice at home (the drill doesn't require hitting a ball), and have perfect tempo the next time you play.

BACKSWING

Swing the club to the top of your backswing and bring your left foot back to touch your right. The feet should now be together.

DOWNSWING

Spread your feet apart before starting your downswing.

FINISH

Swing through to a complete finish position and then bring the right foot forward to touch the left. Both feet should be together at this finish position.

Repeat the drill, feeling the rhythm of the swing. If it helps to count out loud for each stepping of the feet, by all means do so.

Making Shots

GOLF SWING TIMING

Look at John Daly's driving sequence. This is a great example of timing and tempo that works for him even though John's club goes way beyond parallel at the top of his backswing. His tempo and timing bring the clubhead back to the ball in a very smooth sequence.

T

TRANSITION

Once you reach a good position at the top of your backswing, you should have very few problems with the rest of your swing. Provided, of course, that you know how to start your transition back to the ball. Beginning it incorrectly with just your arms takes the club outside the target line; the club will slice across the ball at impact, producing uncontrollable left-to-right curving ball flight—a slice. Transitions correctly begin from the ground up.

Tom Lehman expertly demonstrates his transition philosophy, and Martin Hall has a backyard drill sure to help your transition get off to the right start.

Tom Lehman's transition begins his powerful free-flowing return to the ball.

THE EIFFEL TOWER

If I were to start coaching a beginner I would work the hardest on making sure they were at the correct position at the top of their backswing. Once you get there it's just a reaction to begin the transition and hit the ball.

The key is arriving to the top with a solid base, like the Eiffel Tower in Paris. It's solid and supports the turn. Once you get in this position, properly balanced and wound up, it's time to release the energy back to the ball.

✔ CHECKLIST
TRANSITION

✔ Work on the amount your shoulders have turned versus how much your hips have turned. You need power, and if the hips resisted on the backswing while your upper body stayed connected all the way to the top, you have plenty to fuel the transition.

✔ Keep your weight on your right side (left side for left-handers).

✔ Maintain your head position in the center of your swing.

✔ Keep your spine vertical without tilting.

✔ Do not sway outside your right leg.

TOM'S TRANSITION

Tom begins the transition with his lower body.

The first sequence of movement that begins the return to the ball starts with my left hip and left knee. The best of both worlds is having them moving together. You can see that in the photos above.

Thinking in terms of returning the left hip and left knee to their original position at address is a good swing thought. The clubhead's downward movement in the photos above is caused strictly by the hip and knee motion, not a release of the arms. This lower body motion pulls the clubhead down to the correct path. You must have this move to play good golf!

MARTIN'S TIGHT STRING TRANSITION DRILL

PGA TOUR professionals have effortless looking golf swings because they have no slack in any part of it, especially the transition. The key to this drill is keeping the string tight as you begin your transition. You only need some string or rope and a loop that can be anchored into the ground, to perfect this vital swing movement.

Martin Hall's drill will help you develop perfect lower body transition in your backyard.

1- ANCHOR THE LOOP

This corkscrew with a loop can be found in pet stores. It's used to anchor a dog's backyard play rope.

2- TIE THE KNOT

Tie one end of a rope or twine to a left-side belt loop.

3- THREAD THE ROPE

Run the other end of the rope through the loop anchored to the ground.

4- SET THE TIGHTNESS

Swing to the top of a partial backswing without a club, taking up the extra rope and eliminating the slack. The rope should be tight.

5- ADDRESS POSITION

At the address position, keep the slack from the properly measured rope in your hand. That's okay at this point of the swing.

6- BACKSWING

Rotating to the top of your partial backswing should once again take up the slack. In both of these views, you can see how tight the rope is.

7- NO SLACK TRANSITION

Notice how the left hip and left knee began the transition. The rope remains tight because the arms have not moved downward before the lower body rotated. The only movement is the lower body pulling them down.

8- INCORRECT SLACK

The arms moved first, and you can see the slack in the rope. Practice this drill at home, and work on taking the slack out of your transition.

T

TRIANGLE

This photo shows the triangle formed by Tom Lehman's hands, arms and shoulders at the very top of his backswing. This is a connected swing that keeps the club's grip in front of the chest at all positions.

Practice on the range with that thought in mind and your timing should improve. Professionals' easy-looking, fluid swings are a result of eliminating any extraneous motion to get back on path. Keeping everything together creates the harmony so evident in the TOUR pros' swings.

Tom Lehman's shoulders, arms and hands are in a relative triangle connection during all positions in his golf swing.

UNEVEN LIES
DOWNHILL AND UPHILL

When the ball is above or below your feet, just remember this simple tip: Set your spine alignment to form a 90-degree angle with the slope. Failing to modify your address will result in either thinned or fat shots, depending on the slope plane.

Club selection plays an equally important role for mastering this shot, and again the concept is simple: Take more loft for downhill shots and less loft for uphill shots.

Here's why: Downhill lies fight getting the ball airborne while uphill lies launch it too high. These are just a few of the tips offered by Tom Lehman and Martin Hall.

DOWNHILL LIES

An inherent problem of downhill lies is getting the ball airborne. Swinging downhill and getting the ball to climb requires several adjustments.

DOWNHILL SHOT INSIDE 100 YARDS

I'll demonstrate how to play the shot, and Martin Hall shows you how to practice it. My goal, in the photo at left, is making adjustments from my normal game to encourage a higher ball flight from this downhill lie.

First and foremost is selecting a more-lofted club than I would normally use from this distance. In this case a lob wedge. Here are some other changes to make to your setup:

• Position the ball slightly back in your stance.

• Open the club slightly before gripping as a compensation for the ball position.

• Aim left of the target.

• Put your weight on your downhill foot.

• Verify that your spine is perpendicular (90 degrees) to the slope.

Use a lob wedge (inset), position the ball back in your stance, and aim left of your target.

✔ CHECKLIST
DOWNHILL LIES

✔ Select a more-lofted club.

✔ Play the ball back in a slightly open stance.

✔ Align the spine, forming a 90-degree angle to the slope.

✔ Make several practice swings to feel your balance.

✔ Swing along the slope line.

U

ADDING LOFT/INCREASING BOUNCE

Tom made two adjustments that are directly related—he positioned the ball back in his stance and opened the face of his lob wedge. Any time you play the ball back in your stance loft is subtracted; in this case, where loft is critical for the success of the shot, he added more loft by opening the face. Always remember to adjust the face prior to gripping, but be on alert for a potential problem.

Opening the face of a wedge that already has bounce in it adds additional bounce. This can cause the club to skip off the ground, skulling the shot. Consult a club technician about customizing your clubs for the way you use them. This may require grinding off some bounce.

QUIET LOWER BODY

Notice how Tom's lower body remains in balance through impact as he rotates around his spine.

Setting the weight on my left foot at address provides the balance to turn around my perpendicular-to-the-slope spine position without changing my posture. Regardless if your downhill shot is a long or short one, maintaining this balanced position guards against skulling the ball.

Precise impact between clubface and ball is needed to get the ball airborne, and rotating around a fixed spine encourages that.

COMPLETE FOLLOW-THROUGH

Always follow through to a complete finish position for downhill shots. High follow-throughs encourage high trajectories, and from a downhill lie that's just what you need.

PERPENDICULAR: THE ONLY ANGLE

Martin Hall demonstrates how to properly set up for downhill shots.

Your left or downhill leg is the brace that provides stability for this down-the-slope shot. The key is to set up and verify that your spine alignment is perpendicular to the slope.

Take your stance holding your club (I'm using a pole to demonstrate) in front so that a 90-degree angle is formed with the slope. Then match your spine to the club. Maintaining this angle automatically helps you swing down the slope line.

UPHILL LIES

Uphill lies make getting the ball high in the air too easy. Shots that fly too high end up short. My adjustments are made to lower the trajectory.

UPHILL LIE INSIDE 100 YARDS

Use a less-lofted club and swing along the slope line.

Making a smooth swing that follows the uphill terrain is the key ingredient for playing this shot successfully. The challenge is lowering the trajectory to reach the green.

Setting up is extremely important, along with proper club selection. Because a slope increases the loft of a club, compensate with a less-lofted selection.

SET UP FOR SUCCESS

By selecting a less-lofted pitching wedge to replace the sand wedge, I now have enough club to reach the green for this 90-yard shot. Now comes the setup. Instead of separately thinking about setting my shoulders and hips parallel to the slope, just setting with my spine perpendicular to the ground angle aligns all my body parts at the same time.

One other adjustment to further decrease clubhead loft: position the ball slightly back in your stance. Practicing this shot helps determine the correct ball position.

Tom's spine is perpendicular to the slope line. That automatically aligns his key body parts to the slope. Notice it creates 90-degree angles with his shoulders and hips.

DOWNSWING THROUGH IMPACT

Tom swings along the slope line (1-3), creating the perfect trajectory for this uphill shot.

Uphill lies offer plenty of elevation for launching the ball, so my downswing must bring the club into the ball following the ground line. I even continue following it past impact so as not to increase clubhead loft.

Good shots can only be struck by rotating around a fixed spine angle. Mine stays at 90 degrees. Good geometry creates good golf. Had he played, Euclid had the intelligence to be a world-class golfer.

U

QUICK FOLLOW-THROUGH

Your follow-through must be rapid to achieve a lower trajectory. While you may never have learned this tip before, it's imperative to playing this shot successfully.

The highlights of this abrupt finish position are that your hands are opposite your face and the clubhead is pointing to the target.

AVOID CREATING TOO MUCH LOFT

SPINE PERPENDICULAR = CORRECT TRAJECTORY

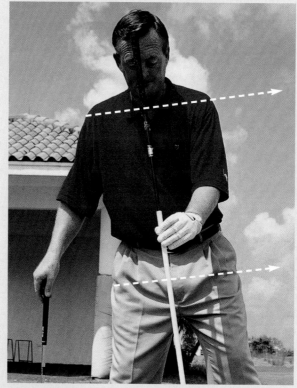

You'll get good trajectory from this spine angle.

INCORRECT SPINE POSITION = TRAJECTORY TOO HIGH

The ball will fly high from this spine angle.

For both uphill and downhill lies your spine alignment angle must be perpendicular to create a 90-degree angle with the ground. As you address the ball, hold a club in front set to the correct angle; then, if needed, adjust your spine angle to match it.

As you can see in the bottom photo, the incorrect angle incorrectly places your body ahead of the club, setting the shoulder and hip lines pointing higher. Consequently, ball flight will be too high. That's not what you need when hitting uphill.

SIDEHILL LIES

Lies below or above your feet require a different group of adjustments. Now the emphasis shifts to adjustments geared more toward correcting potential off-target line shots.

These uneven lie shots want to go more in the direction of the sloping ground, so compensations need to be made. If you're a right-hander this means lies above your feet want to fly more toward the left and balls below your feet more to the right. Reverse both effects for left-handed golfers. Tom and Martin have shotmaking tips for playing both these shots successfully.

Sidehill lies are tough!

BELOW YOUR FEET LIES

✔CHECKLIST
LIES BELOW YOUR FEET:

✔ Play the ball back in your stance.

✔ Aim slightly to the left to compensate for the ball's tendency to drift to the right.

✔ Do not bend the knees at address; bend from the waist.

✔ Put weight more on the heels.

✔ Maintain balance through a complete follow-through.

When you find yourself in this downhill slope position, take Tom's advice to compensate for the ball drifting off the target line.

MARTIN'S SHOTMAKING TIPS

AMOUNT OF DRIFT

Does the ball drift the same amount for shots both above and below your feet? No, the amount of drift is not the same for both shots.

The amount of draw (above your feet) is greater than the amount of fade (below your feet). Higher-lofted clubs drift more than less-lofted clubs. Take this into consideration when you set up for lies below or above your feet.

HIT MORE INTO THE HILL

Aim slightly into the hill to compensate for downhill drift.

This ball is below my feet but a careful look at the photo above shows one of the changes made from playing level shots. I'm actually aiming slightly into the hill as compensation for the ball wanting to drift downhill off the target line.

Bending more from the waist sets the needed amount of knee flex, correctly placing the weight on the back of my heels for balance.

U

DOWNSWING, IMPACT AND FOLLOW-THROUGH

DOWNSWING

The natural loft of the club does the work by allowing it to slip under the ball. Notice my downswing follows the slope and how quickly the ball got airborne.

A high, complete follow-through features my right foot pivoting and pointing toward the target. Hitting more into the slope keeps this shot more balanced and accurate.

Club slips under the ball …

IMPACT   FOLLOW-THROUGH

… for a good hit followed by a high, complete follow-through.

MARTIN'S DOWNSLOPE SUGGESTIONS

With the ball below your feet grip the club all the way to the end of the butt to help compensate for the ball being farther away. Bending from the waist, instead of the knees, sets the correct spine angle and encourages a better-balanced position throughout your swing.

Martin Hall sets more spine alignment angle for downhill side-slope lies.

UPHILL SIDE-SLOPE LIES

As a result of some early bad experiences, I've learned how to correctly play this shot. For a time I thought you had to play a fade to compensate for the natural tendency to hit a draw when the ball is above your feet. Now I know better and play the slope's curvature.

✔ CHECKLIST
LIES ABOVE YOUR FEET

✔ Aim more to the right and choke down on the club.

✔ Play the ball more in the middle of your stance.

✔ Rock back and forth to find your correct balance.

✔ Make a partial swing under the ball.

✔ Finish abruptly with your hands opposite your face for the correct trajectory.

PLAY THE HILL'S CONTOUR

When I used to play a fade to combat the tendency to draw a ball above my feet, the club would steeply impact the hill, creating a fat shot.

I learned a better way. Choke down on the club, because the ball is closer than normal, and aim more to the right, allowing for the natural right-to-

Play with the hill, not against it. Use the contour to your advantage.

left flight. The ball is positioned in the middle of my stance. Rock back and forth slowly until you find a point that feels just right.

REMAIN BALANCED

Tom's balance allows him to launch the ball on the correct trajectory.

All swings must be smooth, but especially those when balance is so critical and difficult to maintain. Following a partial backswing to stay in control, I want to slip the club under the ball for shorter shots, following the contour of the side slope. For longer shots my swing will be more rounded since an upright swing would descend into the hill.

ABRUPT FOLLOW-THROUGH

Finishing with your hands opposite your face helps maintain your balance throughout your swing. No reason to over-swing.

DRILL

MARTIN'S ROUNDED SWING DRILL

Tom referred to a rounded swing. How should that differ from your normal one? Mainly in the balance point. Your normal swing should have the weight over the laces of your shoes. *The rounded swing places the weight more on your heels,* causing the swing to become more rounded than vertical. This drill develops that feeling.

Use a range practice tee with the ball side raised to simulate an above-the-feet lie. If your range does not have one of these, you can tee the ball up and use an iron. Keep the weight on your heels for a partial feel of this shot.

- *Set up with the weight on your heels and choke down on the club (only slightly if the ball is teed up).*

- *Make a three-quarter backswing and swing down and through, matching your backswing and follow-through positions.*

- *Stay in balance as you feel the weight on the back of your heels during the swing.*

- *Replicate this feeling on the course and you will avoid chunking your uphill side-slope shots.*

U

155

UPRIGHT SWING

Upright swing planes promote accurate high-trajectory shots. The key is in returning the clubhead square to the target line at impact. Let's watch Chi Chi Rodriguez do it right.

COMPARE THE BACKSWINGS

STEEPER BACKSWING   *SHALLOWER BACKSWING*

See the amount of vertical difference in two of Chi Chi's backswings. The left one can easily be identified as the upright backswing.

This 9 o'clock position is the desired length for an upright swing plane.

The upright swing is primarily made with a shorter club, since a high trajectory is the desired result. So stand closer to the ball, as Chi Chi Rodriguez is; this encourages an upright swing plane.

It's imperative that the clubhead loft, set at address, be retained at impact. Only a clubface square to the target line can produce the accuracy and loft needed. A correct swing plane is vitally important to success.

SQUARE AT IMPACT

At the exact moment of impact, notice the square-to-the-target line position of Chi Chi's wedge. You can also see the clubhead loft maintained by duplicating his address position. The only difference is his slightly open hips; they allow the arms to swing through, keeping the club on plane.

FINISH HIGH

All high-trajectory shots must include a high finish follow-through. The length of the follow-through in this case is high but it also matches the length of Chi Chi's backswing.

✔ CHECKLIST
UPRIGHT SWING

✔ Do a slow shoulder take-away.

✔ Keep the triangle formed by the lines of the shoulders, arms and hands intact throughout the swing.

✔ Point your toe to the target at the top of a 9 o'clock backswing.

✔ Impact should closely resemble address.

✔ Follow-through should finish high and swing must follow a slightly inside-to-square to slightly-inside target path.

V's

One look at the hands gripping the club and good instructors quickly observe a telltale sign that betrays the secret problems of a student's game even before they swing. It's the V's—the angles formed between the thumb and forefinger of each hand as it grips the club.

V's indicate the position of the hands gripping the club, and that position directly translates into the position of the clubhead at impact.

HOOKERS' GRIP— TOO STRONG

SLICERS' GRIP— TOO WEAK

NEUTRAL GRIP— JUST RIGHT

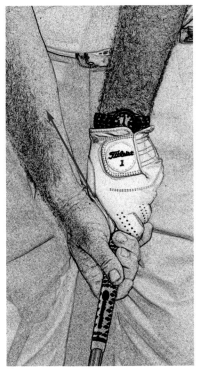

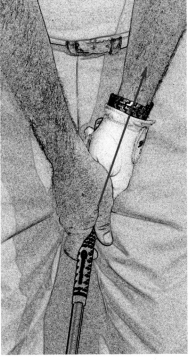

The V's are pointing outside the right shoulder for this right-handed golfer (arrow). Referred to as an overly strong grip, hooking will be the result as the clubface closes at impact. Left-handed hookers have V's that point outside their left shoulder.

Notice how the V of the right hand is pointing to the left shoulder (arrow). This mistake at address will cause the clubface to be open at impact and the ball will slice. Slicing left-handers can identify the problem when the V of their left hand is pointing to their right shoulder.

Correctly gripping the club encourages swinging the club on the proper path. The V's should be pointing between: the chin and right shoulder for right-handers (arrows); the chin and left shoulder for left-handers.

VISUALIZATION

Your brain is a computer. Program it with junk and your golf shots will be junk. Program it with a vision of what you want the ball to do and the results will surprise you.

Think of the rocks, pull out an old ball from your bag, and your brain will make sure you never find that ball again after you hit it. But stand confidently on the tee, visualizing your new ball flying on a perfect trajectory and feeling the tempo of the swing you need before confidently stepping in. Most likely you'll be pulling out your putter for the next shot!

Tom Lehman successfully plays this shot because he visualized it properly even before addressing the ball.

SHAPE VISUALIZATION

As Scott McCarron stands behind the tee box, he's visualizing the ball flying to his target even before teeing it up. Preferring to think only of getting the ball to the target, McCarron pre-programs his brain before he even steps in ... visualizing his ball flying on the exact power fade line he chose.

PUTTING VISUALIZATION

Jack Nicklaus was, and still is, a master at visualization. He would visualize the ball flying to his target off the tee, see it land at the exact chosen spot on the green and react the way he wanted. He even visualized his putts rolling along his target line to the hole and then rolling back along that same line to his putter. His incredible record validates this positive mental approach to golf.

VISUALIZE A PUTTING HIGHWAY

Try this visualization tip to improve your putting. Visualize your ball resting in the middle lane representing the path you selected to the hole. Now stroke your ball so it stays in that lane as it rolls. This helps ensure your putter face is square at impact, sending the ball accurately along the target path to the hole.

Your mind can create a highway to the hole.

WAGGLE

Waggle: "A preliminary swinging of the golf clubhead back and forth over the ball before the swing." —Webster's Dictionary.

Waggle: "It's much easier to begin a fluid backswing from a little bit of motion than from dead silence." —Tom Lehman.

Think about the simplicity of Tom's version of the waggle and compare that with the number of times you've watched your buddies be totally motionless for an agonizing period of time before starting their backswing. Are you guilty of the same lack of pre-swing movement?

PGA TOUR professionals all have a pre-shot routine, and while we show a few earlier in this book, all feature waggles. But the *number* of waggles varies widely. John Daly prefers three waggles and then starts, but Tom employs five waggles to start the rhythm of his swing.

TOM'S WAGGLES

Watch me during a tournament and count the waggles. You will see five every time because I've found they help get the rhythm of my swing started. While it's not exactly put to music, I sense a five-count before I take it away.

TOM SAYS:

Hal Sutton may be the exception to the waggle rule. He begins his swing from a dead stop. But most of us have a little bit of waggle in our swing, or at least a forward press. Some players even include a partial backswing motion to program the swing arc.

Actually, you will find my real swing initiator is a slight forward press following the five waggles. Do you need five waggles? The only honest answer anyone can give you is to experiment with a pre-shot routine that includes the number of waggles that best help your game. But get some motion into the clubhead before bringing it back.

JOHN DALY: THREE LOOKS, THREE WAGGLES AND GO!

John Daly incorporates three looks and three waggles into his pre-shot routine. The reason? "When I first came on TOUR it was two looks and two waggles, but I needed to slow down a little so I increased each to three."

Look at the target, one.

Waggle one.

Look at the target, two.

Waggle two.

Look at the target, three.

Waggle three.

After three looks and three waggles, the shot is off!

WEDGES

Wedges are for accuracy, not distance. Within the 50- to 100-yard range, wedges are the primary club played. Some PGA TOUR professionals carry three wedges in their bag while others, like Tom Lehman, usually carry only two.

THE THREE WEDGES

PITCHING OR GAP WEDGE

Pitching wedges, and their cousins the gap wedges, are for longer shots, although both can also be used close to the green for chipping and pitching. This wedge features 48 degrees of loft and eight degrees of bounce on average.

SAND WEDGE

Played out of bunkers but also for approach shots, sand wedges provide 56 degrees of loft and 12 degrees of bounce. Many TOUR players remove a portion of the bounce (the area of the club that extends below the leading edge), fine tuning it for their games.

LOB WEDGE

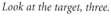

With 60 degrees of loft, the lob wedge is used closer to the green and is the ideal club for hitting a high-flying, soft-landing shot over a hazard while keeping the ball close to the pin. Some lob wedges can have 62 degrees of loft along with three degrees of bounce.

TOUR PROFESSIONALS' WEDGE DISTANCES

Lob Wedge   Sand Wedge   Pitching Wedge

PGA TOUR and SENIOR PGA TOUR players know how far they can hit each of their clubs. The closer they get to the hole, the more vital that knowledge becomes. They are in the hunt for eagles and birdies, so their mindset once they pull a wedge from the bag is to hole the shot, not just get it close. Here are pros' average maximum distances for each.

PROS

Pitching wedge=125 yards with a full swing.

Sand wedge=105 yards (full swing), 85 yards (three-quarter swing).

Lob wedge=65-70 yards.

AMATEUR WEDGE DISTANCES

For comparative purposes, here are the average maximum distances amateurs can effectively play the three wedges. Pardon the irreverence for the lob wedge, but the fact is many amateurs encounter difficulty in mastering this lofted club consistently.

AMATEURS

Pitching wedge=70 to 100 yards.

Sand wedge=55 to 80 yards.

Lob wedge=Under 50 yards, but can also be -5 to 80 yards depending if they slid the face under the ball, stubbed the club or skulled the shot.

BOUNCE

Bounce is the portion of a sand wedge that extends below the leading edge. It's the flange on the back of the club. When a PGA TOUR professional lays his sand wedge open it looks very flat compared to yours. Here's why:

Gene Sarazen designed a sand iron with bounce to create a cushion of sand that propels the ball out of a bunker. But sand wedges can also be outstanding clubs to use around the green. Have a professional clubmaker in your area remove some of that bounce by grinding it to the amount that works best for you both in the sand and around the green.

Professionals remove some of the bounce to make the sand wedge more versatile.

TOM'S SHOTMAKING TIPS

TOM'S VIEWS ON BOUNCE

Carrying two wedges is my normal club selection for most events. You can always add loft or take loft off with any club, so if I have a shot that needs to go a little bit higher and land softer I open the face, which adds the loft.

That's why it's important to pay attention to the bounce in your club. If you have too much bounce already built in, that increases when you open the blade. Anytime you increase loft you also increase bounce, with it increasing the probability of skulling the shot. So if you're frustrated trying to emulate a professional's laid-open wedge shot you saw on TV, that may be the reason.

I like to play most of my wedge shots with just one club, so it's important to get the right bounce into it. I have 12 degrees of bounce in my 56-degree wedge. It's a little too much but you have to have *some* bounce in the sand when playing a fairway shot.

When you play the shot farther forward in your stance you are also adding more bounce, so you need to understand the way the club works. If you have no bounce (like Phil Mickelson) you can play it way up and get away with it, but if you have a lot of bounce you will find the results will not be satisfactory.

W

TAILOR YOUR GRIP FOR THE SHOT

The wedge's versatility can be enhanced by the way you grip the club. PGA TOUR professionals often use two distinct grips to enhance their wedge shotmaking abilities. Martin Hall demonstrates each with some tees as instructional aids.

FULL SWING GRIP

PARTIAL SHOT FINESSE GRIP

When you must play a full swing wedge, use the same grip you use when driving the ball. As you look down, the V's of both hands should be at 1 o'clock on the ball side and pointing between your right shoulder and chin on your body side.

This strong grip works perfectly on the full swing because of its tendency to close the face of the club slightly, helping square the clubface at impact. Square-to-the-target-line clubfaces translates into accuracy.

High-level wedge play calls for shots requiring less than a full swing. These partial shots need the finesse grip. Weaken your hands (moving them to the left of the grip) so the tees are pointed more toward the top of the shaft and the middle of your body.

To finesse the grip to suit your individual needs, move your hands so the tees line up between the 11:00 and 12:30 positions.

The finesse grip has an advantage for the partial swings: It has an ability to enhance the desirable slice/spin that stops the ball quickly.

✔CHECKLIST
WEDGE PLAY

✔ Stay in control instead of trying to hit a shot farther than the club is capable. Have the right concept of wedge trajectories.

✔ Choke down on the club whenever you play less than a full shot. The shorter the shot the less you want your body involved.

✔ Set up more open to the ball.

✔ Maintain rhythm and balance through the swing.

✔ Never decelerate during a wedge swing.

TOM'S SHOTMAKING TIPS

WEAKER GRIPS

The weaker you grip your wedge, the less hand action you will have involved with the shot. Johnny Miller prefers a really weak grip, feeling that it keeps as little clubface rotation involved as possible.

He wants the clubface to stay as square as possible for as long as possible. Weak grips help promote that while stronger grips (with the V's pointed more toward the right side of the body) allow you to work your hands through impact. The reason? The more curving you have on the shot, the less consistency you will have.

TOM'S FULL WEDGE SWING

When I make several birdies in a round, I'll guarantee my wedge play was responsible for half of them. Here in the next few pages you can come inside the ropes for a close-up view of my full wedge swing and see it from a variety of angles. Along the way I'll point out some important checkpoints to help you better understand how to play this scoring club.

1- SETUP

Stand up to the ball and bending slightly from the waist, making it easy to turn around your straight spine. Open your stance slightly to the target line.

2- TAKE-AWAY

A wide swing arc is equally as important for wedge play as it is for driving. Begin with a one-piece take-away consisting of hands, arms and shoulders. The grip of the club will remain in front of your chest, although the butt of the grip will not remain pointed directly at you during the swing.

3- TOE IN THE AIR

A good checkpoint to verify you are tracking the club along the correct swing plane is when the arms reach the parallel-to-the-ground position. At this point the toe of the club should be pointing up. Problems occur if it's pointing across the target line (that means it's incorrectly closed) or pointing behind you (indicating it is incorrectly open).

4- 9 O'CLOCK POSITION

You can see the toe is pointed correctly in the air. The extension seen in the left arm indicates you're working along a wide swing arc. You may not be able to straighten your arm out as far as this but get it extended as far as you can. This would also be the top of the backswing position for a partial shot.

5- TOP OF THE BACKSWING

Unlike the long game swing, you do not need to get the club to a parallel-to-the-ground position on your backswing. This is as far as you need to go. The tempo of the swing is not fast but controlled. The last thing you want is a wild, uncontrolled backswing when accuracy is your goal. A checkpoint: Your back should face the target.

W

6- Transition

7- Pre-Impact

Stay behind the ball and rotate around a steady spine. The head is the center of the swing so it remains in place. The wrists have not released and the clubhead is approaching the ball along a slightly inside path, indicating the club is on the correct swing plane.

In this combined action photo showing a down-the-line view of the top of the backswing and move back toward the ball, you see the essence of a good golf swing. Tom's head has not moved even though momentum is building quickly.

The rotation of knees and hips back toward the target led the transition and pulled the upper body down to this point. Resist with the lower body as you wind up, but let the lower body lead the way back to the ball.

8- Impact

Weight should properly transfer over to the side closest to the target (left side for right-handers and right side for left-handers). The spine remains steady and does not slide forward. Any movement affects the accuracy and ball trajectory. This is not a high backspin shot so the wrists do not release through the ball.

9- Past Impact

Never decelerate when you hit a wedge. This looks like a power position. Notice the head position remains fixed. The shoulders will rotate it upward naturally. At this point it's important to stay on plane and not swing the club too much to the inside. The reason? What you see at this point is set up by pre-impact motion, and if the club were too inside at this point it would have approached the ball from the outside and the clubhead would not have impacted the ball square to the target line.

10- Follow-Through

For a full wedge shot, follow through facing the target. If you finished facing in any other direction, accuracy would have been adversely affected by something that happened earlier in the swing. Remember, never decelerate when playing a wedge. For a full wedge always follow through to this point.

9 O'Clock Backswing

Bruce Fleisher's phenomenal SENIOR PGA TOUR rookie season was made possible by the time he spent working on his wedges and putting for several years leading up to his debut. His outstanding wedge accuracy is built around a controllable 9 o'clock backswing.

Bruce's key for achieving consistent distances with his wedges is his 9 o'clock backswing. His arms are pointed to that clock position for his arm-dominated backswing.

Bruce makes a normal follow-through and finishes facing the target even though he used an abbreviated backswing.

9 O'Clock Yardage

Bruce Fleisher's partial backswing delivers the following yardage for each of his three wedges:

Club	Yardage
49-degree pitching wedge	100 yards
56-degree sand wedge	80 yards
60-degree lob wedge	60 yards

Weight Shift

Weight transfer in the golf swing translates into power. Starting with a 50/50 weight distribution for the full swing, the weight follows the direction of the clubhead, moving back on the backswing and forward on the downswing. Pretty simple!

So why is improper weight transfer one of the most common mistakes amateur golfers make? Because, according to Tom Lehman, the most difficult thing about golf is trying to teach someone to do that naturally.

Having the correct mental image helps.

W

THE REVERSE WEIGHT SHIFT

Below I show the classic reverse weight shift, or as it's usually referred to, *reverse pivoting*, in front of a stake that initially was lined up with the spine. The word "reverse" indicates that the weight is on the wrong side of the body at the wrong time.

Seen here, weight shift is incorrectly on the left side during the backswing (1) and incorrectly transfers to the right side past impact (2). So instead of the power being transferred into the ball, you fall away. That costs yards and accuracy.

CORRECT WEIGHT SHIFTING

After I set up to the ball with a 50/50 weight distribution, my swing begins. As you can see in the two photos below, I load up the weight totally on my right side on the backswing.

The role of the backswing, other than to take the club away from the ball, is to coil and store up energy. The downswing is the process of moving your weight to the left side and releasing that stored-up energy.

Tom's weight follows his clubhead: away from the target on the backswing, toward the target on the downswing. He finishes with all his weight on his target-side foot.

STAYING CENTERED

Let's discuss correcting weight shifting but substitute the term *tilting* instead. Your spine needs to stay vertical as you turn around it. But if you reverse weight shift you tilt your spine one way and then the other.

Correct weight shifting centers around not *moving* your spine but *turning* around it. Learning to keep your center in the same spot while turning around it may be the most important and significant thing you can do to consistently play better golf.

CENTERED AT ADDRESS

The pole is lined up with the center of the spine at address.

Compare the spine positions in relationship to the pole in both photos. In the main photo, showing the backswing's correct weight transfer to the right side, the spine remains vertical. In the inset photo there is tilting and the weight is on the wrong side of the body.

At follow-through in the main photo, weight has transferred over to the left side. But in the inset photo the weight went to the right side and away from the target. The key is not to tilt when you turn. Instead, keep your spine vertical and centered as you turn around it.

WRISTS

During the golf swing the wrists can be in one of nine positions:

1 - Flat

2 - Arched

3 - Bent

4 - Level

5 - Cocked

6 - Uncocked

7 - Turned

8 - Vertical

9 - Rolled

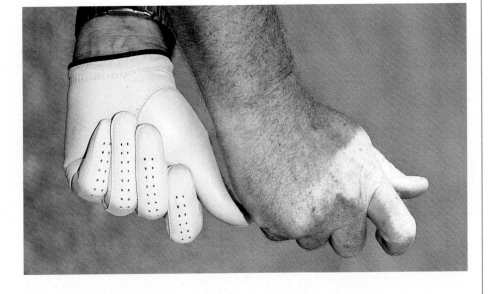

Look at Tom Lehman's wrists at three key positions during his swing and see how the positions change.

SETUP

Tom's wrists are:

- Left wrist bent, level and vertical.

- Right wrist flat, level and vertical.

TAKE-AWAY

Tom's wrists are:

- Left wrist flat, turned and cocked.

- Right wrist bent, turned and cocked.

IMPACT

Tom's wrist positions will be opposite of what they were at setup.

- Left wrist flat, level and vertical.

- Right wrist bent, level and vertical.

W

Z Factor

A scuba diver surfaces with one of the many balls that fell victim to the clutches of Bay Hill's notorious 18th hole, which is dubbed "The Devil's Bathtub." The Z factor contributes to many watery demises. This section shows how to combat it.

Lee Trevino jokes about "soldier golf" some amateurs play—left-right, left-right. That's the Z FACTOR. This section deals with how to eliminate it.

World Golf Village in St. Augustine, Florida, is home to the World Golf Hall of Fame. If it had a separate wing for golf tips, the most illustrious inductee would be: **Keep the ball in play.** Simple to understand, but for many golfers hard to do. Is there anything more frustrating than seeing a beautiful golf hole in front of you and not being able to enjoy it because you're either searching for a ball in the woods or saw it drop into the pond?

Golf course architects want you to admire their work, but they didn't expect you to visit every remote location on a hole. **Grid Target Golf** is the way to eliminate this problem and cut strokes off your game regardless of your handicap. Here's what Grid Target Golf can do for you:

- Save strokes before you even tee off.

- Take advantage of your current game.

- Look at the golf hole like never before.

- Stay out of trouble as you eliminate penalty shots.

LOOK AT THE HOLE

Before you even tee up, take a really good look at the hole. Many scorecards have a diagram or you can purchase a yardage book at the pro shop. Using Arnold Palmer's Bay Hill Club's notorious 18th hole as an example, we'll show you how to customize Grid Target Golf for your current game.

Look at the hole before you tee up and whack a ball.

THE REAL OBJECTIVE

Grid Target Golf teaches you to keep your ball in play. It will reduce the high number of penalty shots, usually incurred by mid- to high-handicap golfers, and lower your score. Penalty shots come from lost balls, out of bounds hits and lateral hazards. By just visualizing a grid superimposed on the hole in front of you, and factoring in the shape of your normal shot, you learn where to tee the ball up and how to aim it more effectively.

Grid Target Golf creates scoring opportunities for low-handicap golfers. Depending on the changing variables—such as wind, weather, pin placements and how you're playing that particular day—you can use and rely on Grid Target Golf to provide aiming points to help you adjust.

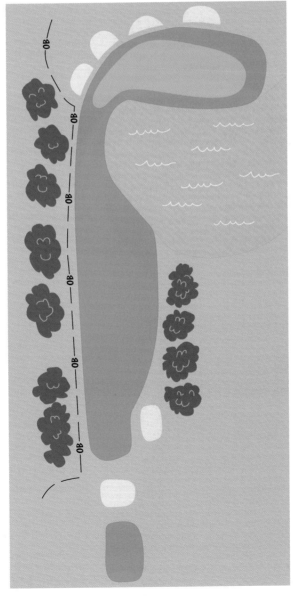

MAPPING YOUR ROUTE

Be honest now, when you looked at the diagram did you mainly look at all the potential trouble, like the lake and out of bounds markers? That's natural, but to start cutting some strokes off your game, look at the hole and its diagram and see **potential opportunity** instead.

A yardage book features a road map to the hole, but you need your own customized map that takes advantage of your current game. As your swing improves, the shape of your shots will change and another route to the hole may be preferable. For illustration purposes, here's how four golfers, with different skill levels, can effectively use it to cut scores.

You need to know the ground. This map: The Par-4, 414-yard 18th hole at Arnold Palmer's Bay Hill Club.

Z

PLAYER A: PROFESSIONAL OR AMATEUR SCRATCH GOLFER

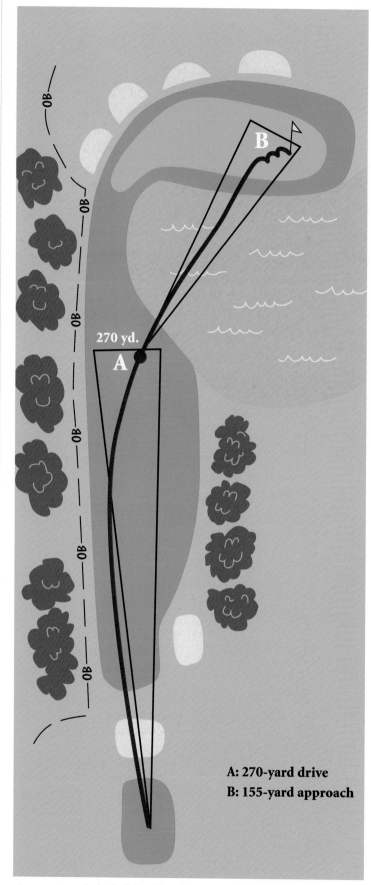

A pro can work the ball in either direction. He chooses to work away from out of bounds right off the tee.

A: 270-yard drive
B: 155-yard approach

A pro would play the hole as shown in this diagram. Bay Hill's traditional difficult Sunday pin placement is shown to make a pro's path to the hole even more precise. During the annual Bay Hill Invitational held each March, the hole is set to the right side of the green on Sunday. A shot that comes up short results in a watery grave, and many a tournament has been lost that way.

Long is not much better. The bunkers behind the green make it difficult to get close to the pin because the green slopes away toward the rocks. But using Grid Target Golf, here's how most pros play the hole.

STRATEGY

Two grids have been drawn in, one for the drive and one for the approach shot. These grids are fairly narrow when compared to the grids for high-handicap amateurs.

- The pro wants his ball in the right center of the fairway off the tee, feeling this provides the best location to hit the second shot to the pin on the right side. This requires hitting a left-to-right fade on the drives. So he starts his ball 10 yards inside the out-of-bounds trouble on the left and fades it back perfectly.

- Using the grid as his guide, the pro tees the ball up at the right center of the tee box and plans on starting the ball outside the left side of the grid, fading it back into the exact landing spot he wants: a 270-yard drive that leaves 155 yards for the approach.

- Instead of seeing the water hazard and wide green ahead, the approach shot grid focuses on a landing area close to the hole. Notice how it provides more room left of the pin. If the pro can land his ball on the green within this grid, he has a good shot at birdie.

- Using the grid as a guide, the pro stays on the left side of the grid and his ball lands and rolls to the middle of the targeted landing area, well within range for a birdie putt.

PLAYER B: LOW-HANDICAP

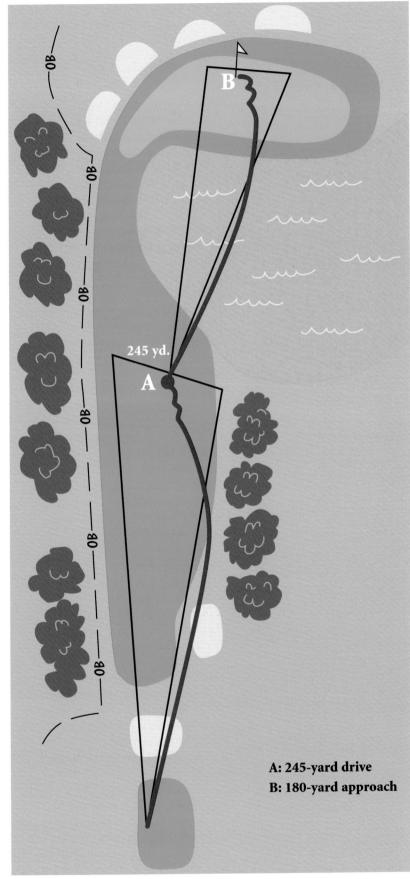

245 yd.

A

B

80
80
80
80
80
80
80

A: 245-yard drive
B: 180-yard approach

The low-handicap player's stock shot is a draw, playing for the middle of the fairway.

Our next player is a low-handicap golfer. He might have a handicap between 5 and 10. A draw, the right-to-left ball movement, is this golfer's stock shot. The pin is now in the central part of the green to make the hole somewhat easier.

STRATEGY

Player B's grid is wider and starts at the fairway's right edge since the preference is to play a draw. Teeing the ball on the far left side of the tee box provides additional fairway to work with.

- Player B wants to take the out of bounds on the left out of play. Aiming at the right side of the grid, knowing the ball won't be able to draw back far enough to go out of bounds, is the plan. Not using the grid and aiming down the center of the fairway, a draw can end up out of bounds, costing a one-stroke penalty.

- The 245-yard drive is safely in the center of the fairway. The grid provided a safe margin of error. Even if Player B had not hit his best shot he would still have finished on the right side of the fairway. A little shorter but still in good shape.

- Player B's second shot is aimed to the right of the grid and draws safely to the middle of the green. Playing a draw into this pin placement is difficult to get really close. As a result, Player B's reasonable expectation is to make par, but birdie remains a possibility.

- Grid Target Golf helped Player B avoid penalty strokes and navigate smartly to have a chance at birdie.

Z

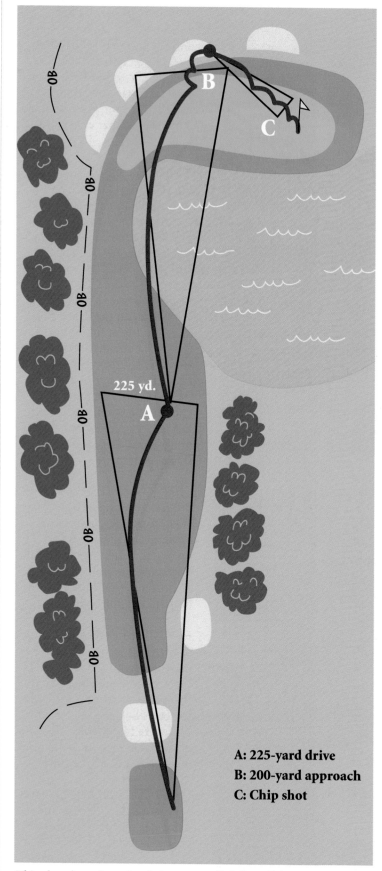

Player C is a mid-handicap (11-20) golfer. As with many players in this category, the fade or a controlled slice is the tendency.

STRATEGY

Player C's tendency to hit shots from left to right suggests visualizing a grid that almost stretches across the complete fairway. Teeing the ball and the aiming direction are extremely crucial to staying out of trouble.

- Player C wisely tees it up on the right side of the tee box, providing the entire left side of the fairway to work with.

- By aiming the shot at the left side of the grid, this player's ball will start to the left but fade back toward the center of the grid 225 yards down the fairway. Even if he didn't hit his best shot, the ball would still be safe in the left center section of the grid.

- Aiming down the center of the fairway, the ball would have faded or sliced into the trees on the right. That would have cost a valuable shot to extricate himself from that predicament rather than use the same stroke to go for the green.

- Being aggressive, this player wants to go for the green instead of laying up. To guarantee success, enough club must be selected to carry the ball to the back of the green. Being short means ... splash!

- The 200-yard approach shot is aimed slightly outside the left grid boundary to give it plenty of room to move back toward the center. The grid was aimed to the left center of the green to help avoid some of the bunkers behind.

- Having a chip shot from the back of the green and the opportunity to get it close enough to putt for a par, or even hole the chip, is a wonderful reward for this aggressive, yet smart, golfer.

225 yd.

A

A: 225-yard drive
B: 200-yard approach
C: Chip shot

This player's tendency is a fade or controlled slice off the tee. He takes plenty of club to carry the back of the green. Chipping back always is a good bailout.

PLAYER D: HIGH-HANDICAP

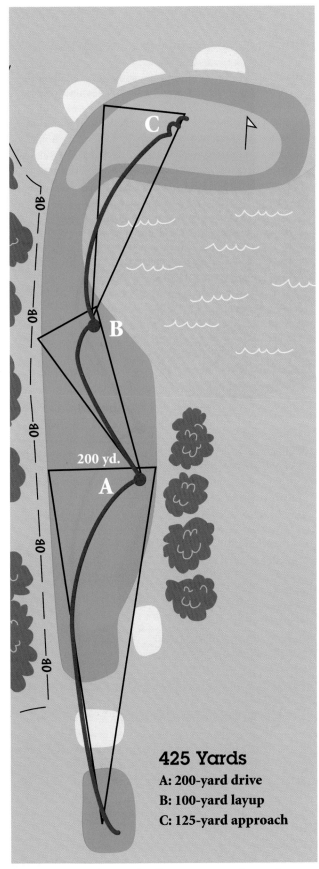

425 Yards
A: 200-yard drive
B: 100-yard layup
C: 125-yard approach

This player is a slicer and puller. He wants to lay up for second shot, saving penalty strokes, and he will use the entire green for third shot.

Our high-handicap Player D (21 and up), like most golfers in this skill category, tends to slice or pull the ball. The grid will be very beneficial if he or she takes the time to plan some strategy and use the grid while playing this challenging hole.

STRATEGY

Losing a ball in the water or having to hit out of the trees is not much fun. Grid Target Golf can help any golfer in this category avoid losing strokes unnecessarily. If this is your category, your goal is making bogey on this hole. You may do better, but bogey would be a good score and is attainable. Stand behind your ball and visualize a grid to help make that a reality.

- Player D's grid extends the full width of the fairway and even the first cut of rough.

- Player D should tee up on the far right side of the tee box to have the entire fairway to work with.

- By aiming to the left side of the grid, which in this case extends to the left edges of the fairway, the ball will sharply slice back to the right but still land in the fairway. See how much room the ball has to work its way back.

- If the grid was not used and Player D aimed at the center of the fairway, the next shot, if the ball were located at all, would be in the trees or the adjoining fairway on the 16th hole. The grid may have saved player D two strokes on the drive (shot A).

- For the second shot, Player D smartly decides to play a 100-yard lay-up shot rather than just hit it as far as possible. The tendency to slice would put the ball in the lake. The grid avoids the "Devil's Bathtub," as the shot is aimed to the left of the grid but slices back to the far right side. The grid provided a safety margin and saved at least one more stroke.

- Faced with a 125-yard approach to the green, Player D's grid is aimed to the center left of the green. The Shot C should be aimed outside the left grid boundary as a safety margin. This actually uses the entire green because player D's slice can actually end up closer to the hole as it slices back in.

- Even with Player D's current game, a chance to make a par on this extremely challenging hole is a wonderful reward for smart play. The grid took into consideration the normal shape tendencies of the shot and the distances Player D can hit various clubs.

Z

GLOSSARY

Address Your body position (posture, alignment, ball position) as you set up to the ball.

Addressing the Ball Taking a stance and grounding the club (except in a hazard) before taking a swing.

Approach A shot hit to the green.

Apron Slightly higher grassy area surrounding the putting surface. Also referred to as fringe.

Away A player who is farthest from the hole. This player plays his or her ball first.

Backspin The spin of a golf ball that is the opposite direction of the ball's flight.

Ball Mark The damaged, indented area in the ground caused by the ball when it lands on the green.

Ball Marker Something small to mark the position of your ball on the putting green. You should leave a marker when you remove your ball both to clean it and also to allow your playing partners to have an unobstructed line to the hole. Markers can be purchased and can be attached to your glove. You may also use a coin or similar object.

Birdie One stroke under the designated par of the hole.

Blade To hit the ball at its center with the bottom edge of your club.

Blocked Shot Hitting a ball on a straight line to the right.

Bogey One stroke over the designated par of the hole.

Bump and Run A type of approach shot that lands and then rolls onto the green and toward the hole.

Bunker Also referred to as a sand trap.

Carry How far a ball flies in the air. If a water hazard is in front of you, you have to figure the carry to be sure you've taken enough club.

Casual Water A temporary water accumulation not intended as a hazard. Consult the published *Rules of Golf* for information on the relief you are entitled to.

Chili-Dip Hitting the ground before contacting the ball. The result: weak, popped-up shots also called "fat."

Divot Turf displaced by a player's club when making a swing. Divots must be repaired.

Double Bogey Two strokes over the designated par for a hole.

Draw A shot that curves from right to left for right-handers and the opposite for left-handed golfers.

Drop The act of returning a ball back into play. Consult *The Rules of Golf* for correct information on circumstances where this occurs.

Eagle Two strokes under the designated par for a hole.

Fade A controlled, slight left-to-right ball flight pattern. Also can be called a cut.

Fairway Closely mowed route of play between tee and green.

Fore A warning cry to any person in the way of play or who may be within the flight of your ball.

Green The putting surface.

Gross Score Total number of strokes taken to complete a designated round.

Ground the Club Touching the surface of the ground with the sole of the club at address.

Halved the Hole The phrase used to describe a hole where identical scores were made.

Handicap A deduction from a player's gross score. Handicaps for players are determined by guidelines published by the USGA.

Honor The right to tee off first, earned by scoring the lowest on the previous hole.

Hook A stroke made by a right-handed player that curves the ball to the left of the target. It's just the opposite for left-handers.

Hosel The metal part of the clubhead where the shaft is connected.

Hot A ball that comes off the clubface without backspin and will go farther than normal as a result. If a lie puts grass between the clubface and ball, the grooves can't grip the ball to develop backspin. Understanding this, a golfer knows the ball will come out "hot" and plans for that.

Lateral Hazard A hazard (usually water) that is on the side of a fairway or green. Red stakes are used to mark lateral hazards.

Lie Stationary position of the ball. It is also described as the angle of the shaft in relation to the ground when the club sole rests naturally.

Local Rules Special rules for the course that you are playing.

Loft The amount of angle built into the clubface.

Match Play A format where each hole is a separate contest. The winner is the individual or team that wins more holes than are left to play.

Mulligan A second ball that's hit from the same location. The shot that's tried again. Limited to friendly, noncompetitive rounds.

Net Score Gross score less handicap.

Par The score a golfer should make on a given hole. Determined by factoring in 2 putts plus the number of strokes needed to cover the yardage between the tee and green.

Provisional Ball A second ball hit before a player looks for his or her first ball, which may be out of bounds or lost.

Pull Shot A straight shot in which the flight of the ball is left of the target for right-handers and right of the target for left-handers.

Push Shot A straight shot in which the flight of the ball is right of the target for a right-handed golfer and left of the target for a left-hander.

Rough Areas of longer grass adjacent to the tee, fairway green or hazards.

Shank To hit a shot off the club's hosel.

Slice A stroke made across the ball, creating spin that curves the ball to the right of the intended target for right-handed golfers and to the left of the target for left-handers.

Stance Position of the feet at address.

Stroke Any forward motion of the clubhead made with an intent to strike the ball. The number of strokes taken on each hole are entered for that hole's score.

Stroke Play Competition based on the total number of strokes taken.

Target The spot or area a golfer chooses for the ball to land or roll.

Top To hit the ball above its center.

INDEX

A

Accuracy
balance and, 18
ball at low spot in swing and, 7, 17
clubface position in swing path, 20–21
club on shoulders drill, 22
four-step drill, 23
hips and, 22
left hand to target drill, 24
long game and, 16–18
open clubface, 113
pitch shots, 113
posture and, 17
putting, 24
scoring zone, 19–23
shoulders and, 22
specific targets for, 16
tempo of swing and, 18
weak wedge grip and, 9
Accuracy drill, 45
Address
chip shots, 111
GAP address, 25–26
90-degree angle in, 25
one-piece take-away, 140–141
pitch shots, 111
shoulders, 135
tips when uncomfortable at, 26
Alignment
GAP address, 26
hips and shoulders in, 27
90-degree angle, 26
tips for checking, 27

B

Backspin, 34–36
creating, 35
defined, 34
limiting, 36
wrists and, 35, 36
Backswing
back to target, 30
checklist for, 28
clubface position in, 20–21
correct backswing image, 31
distance control and, 60
flat or steep swing problem, 31
four-step drill, 23
grip points inside of ball, 30
hips, 29
importance of top of, 8
9 o'clock, 165
order of motion for, 106–107
shoulders, 135
swing plane, 138
toe in air, 30
triangle and, 29, 148
wide swing arc, 28
Balance
accuracy and, 18
drills for, 18
Ball position
chip shots, 111
clubface and, 33
driver, 33
fairway woods, 68
irons, 33
locating position for bottom of swing, 33
at low spot in swing and accuracy, 7, 17
pitch shots, 111
tee height for, 65
Balls
historical perspective on, 32

launch angle and selecting, 105
90 vs. 100 comprehension, 7
Ball spin
backspin, 34–36
sidespin, 34
topspin, 34
Behind the pole drill, 102
Belly wedge, 37
Bounce, 161
Bump and run shot, 38
Bunkers. *See* Sand
Buried lies, 39

C

Centrifugal force, 40–42
developing uninterrupted centrifugal force, 41
little circle/big circle, 41
swing the broom drill, 42
Chip shot, 43–46
accuracy drill, 45
address, 111
ball position, 111
choke down on club, 43
club selection, 45
distance control and club selection, 46
downhill chips, 55
multi-breaking chip, 56
open stance for, 44
vs. pitch shots, 110–111
practice descending hit, 45
putting chip, 54–55
quiet lower body for, 43
rhythmical swing, 44
solid contact setup, 44
wrists, 44
Clap hands drill, 19
Closed clubface, 19, 30, 33, 48
Club distances
average distance for various clubs, 47
calibrating your club distances, 47
middle irons, 100
sweetspot shadow drill, 49
wedges, 161, 165
Clubface
ball position and, 33
closed, 19, 30, 33, 48
clubface position hip high, 20
grip and accuracy, 19
heel hit, 48
hitting sweetspot, 48
hooded clubface, 50
open, 19, 33, 48, 50, 113
square, 19, 48
sweetspot shadow drill, 49
toe hit, 48
Club on shoulders drill, 22
Club selection. *See also* **specific clubs**
chipping and distance control, 46
chip shot, 45
downhill lie pitch, 57
downhill lies, 149
high handicappers, 15
middle handicappers, 15
tips for, 15
Concentration, 51
Connected swing, 52
medicine ball drill, 52
triangle connected drill, 53

D

Delayed impact, 85

Distance control
average distance for various clubs, 47
calibrating your club distances, 47
short game, 60
tips for consistent club distances, 47–49
Divots
interpreting your swing by examining, 63–64
that point left, 64
that point right, 64
Downhill chips, 55
Downhill lie, 149–150
fairway woods, 69
pitch shot, 57
Downswing
distance control and, 60
early stages for, 61
hips, 62
order of motion for, 108
pitch shots, 112
power slot, 62
pre-impact and delayed hit for, 62
swing plane, 138
weight left and, 8
weight transfer, 61
wrists, 62
Draw, 6, 25
checklist for, 133
swing, 133
Driver
average distances for, 47
ball position, 33
choosing best, 15

E

Eyes closed tempo/timing drill, 103

F

Fade, 25
checklist for, 131
follow-through, 72
grip and, 78
high fade shot, 83
swing, 131–132
Fairway entry in journal, 88
Fairway woods
ball position for, 68
checklist for, 68
choosing best, 15
downhill lies, 69
staying behind ball, 69
uphill lies, 69
Feel, 56
Flat swing, 31
Floater, 71
Flob shot, 98–99
Flyer, 126
Follow-through
checklist for, 72
extension positions for, 72–73
grip, 73
for lob shot, 99
order of motion for, 109
pitch shots, 112
shoulders, 135
Four-step drill, 23

G

GAP address
alignment, 26
grip, 25
posture, 26

Goal post drill, 66
Grasses
belly wedge, 37
bentgrass, 74
Bermuda, 74
against the collar shot, 120–123
deep rough shot, 126–127
putting and, 75
reading the grain, 75
Tiff Eagle, 75
Greens entry in journal, 88
Grid Target Golf, 168–173
benefit of, 168
high-handicap, 173
look at hole, 169
low-handicap, 171
mapping route, 169
mid-handicap, 172
objective of, 169
for professional/amateur scratch golfer, 170
Grip
accuracy and, 19
balanced, 76, 79
basic steps for, 77
for beginner, 76–77
clap hands drill, 19
fade and, 78
follow-through, 73
GAP address, 25
hook, 78, 157
interlocking, 76, 78
left hand grip pressure, 79
long thumb, 7, 78
neutral grip, 157
overlapping, 76, 78
putting, 117
putting chip, 54–55
self-diagnosis for, 19
short thumb, 78
slicers grip, 157
strong, 19, 25, 157
two-finger off drill, 79
weak, 9, 25, 157
for wedges, 9, 162

H

Hardpan shot, 80–81
Head, importance of steady, 82
Heel hit, 48, 101
Hips
alignment and, 27
backswing, 29
downswing, 62
knockdown shot, 91
leg drive in, 96–97
one-piece take-away, 140–141
swing path for, 22
Hole the putt speed drill, 67
Hooded clubface, 50
Hook, 6, 48
defined, 34
follow-through, 72
grip, 78, 157
top of backswing and, 21

I

Impact
checklist for, 84
delayed, 85
important elements of, 84
order of motion for, 109
pitch shots, 112
power triangle and, 85
shoulders, 135
unwind drill, 85
Interlocking grip, 76, 78